The Wisdom
of
Personal
Undevelopment

The Wisdom of Personal Undevelopment

The Art of Liberation by Unlearning and Undoing

Mike George

Gavisus Media

The Wisdom of
Personal Undevelopment

Text Copyright Mike George 2018

Print Edition ISBN: 978-0-9933877-3-9

Also available as an E-Book

Published by
Gavisus Media

Email: gavisusmedia@gmail.com

Second Edition
The moral rights of the author have been asserted.

Cover Design: Charlotte Mouncey - www.bookstyle.co.uk

The information given in this book should not be treated as a substitute for professional medical advice; always consult a medical practitioner. Any use of information in this book is at the reader's discretion and risk. Neither the author nor the publisher can be held responsible for any loss, claim or damage arising out of use, or misuse, or the suggestions made or the failure to take medical advice

Other Books by Mike George

BEING BEYOND BELIEF
How to KNOW what is TRUE for YOU!

MINDSETS
Changing your perception and creating new perspectives

The 7 Myths About LOVE...Actually!
The Journey from Your HEAD to the HEART of Your SOUL

BEING Your Self
SEEing and KNOWing What's IN the Way IS the Way!

Don't Get MAD Get Wise
Why no one ever makes you angry...ever!

The Immune System of the SOUL
Freeing Your Self from ALL Forms of Dis - ease

The Journey from IGNORANCE to ENIGHTENMENT
The only journey where you are guaranteed to lose all your baggage.

The 7 AHA!s of Highly Enlightened Souls
How to Free YOUR Self from ALL Forms of Stress

Learn to Find Inner Peace
Manage your anxieties, think well, feel well.

Learn to Relax
Ease tension, conquer stress and free the self

In the Light of Meditation
A guide to meditation and spiritual awakening

Subscribe to CLEAR THINKING

Clear Thinking is a regularly irregular e-article that serves to sustain the ongoing unlearning necessary to increase your self-awareness and self-understanding - to subscribe, go to www.relax7.com.

Dedication

To all those on their way from Mystery to Mastery as they complete their MBA.

Almost everyone acknowledges the mysteries of life whenever they start asking those universal questions such as, "Is this all there is?" and "Why are we here?" and "Why am I doing this?" and "What is my purpose?" and "Why do I feel like this?" and "Who am I anyway?"

The classic signs you are resolving such mysteries and restoring your mastery include:

The restoration of that exhilarating feeling of inner **freedom,** as you are in reality, a free spirit, always.

Greater **clarity** in your encounters with people and circumstances, as you rediscover your own innate wisdom and apply it.

A reclaimed sense of your **power**, not over others, but in your ability to maintain your stability and focus when all around you are in chaos, crisis or confusion.

The road from mystery to mastery is the inner work of the self-awakening, which includes exposing inherited illusions, restoring your true self-awareness and being an inspiration to others as you show them the way.

This book is intended to help you along that road, as you restore your **M**astery of **B**eing **A**ware in all areas of your life.

CONTENTS

INTRODUCTION

In 2005 I arrived in Zagreb for the first time to run a leadership course as a guest facilitator at Cotrugli Business School. We liked each other, the school and I, so I've been returning five or six times each year to run the Executive and Personal Development (PD) module within their MBA programmes, alongside Liberating Leadership workshops and Mindfulness courses for many of the school's clients.

The purpose of this book is to encapsulate the insights, wisdom and practices from the four-day PD module. It will both challenge you to begin your own journey and sustain those who are already on their way.

At the start of the module some participants often say they find it strange that there is such a topic as Personal Development in an MBA programme. After all, the aim of the programme is to have you walk away with an academic qualification in 'business administration', and self-development is not exactly an academic subject. And yet, it's probably the foundation of everything you might hope to achieve with and beyond the achievement of an MBA.

No one teaches us self-understanding and if you don't understand your self you cannot manage your self. If you cannot manage you then you'll likely find it difficult to manage the four R's in every area of your life i.e. your responsibilities, relationships, roles and resources.

Ultimately there are no 'authorities' on PD and it's certainly much more than feeding people with more mechanistic and method based information. The only authority on 'the self' is, ultimately, the self. Only you can develop you or, as the title of this book suggests, undevelop what needs to be undeveloped, in order to be your authentic self and bring the gifts of your true nature and potential into the world.

It's unfortunate that our mainstream education systems seem to place so little emphasis on the cultivation of self-awareness. This is the foundation of self-understanding and self-management. But it's understandable in a world largely shaped and driven by the material paradigm. It's a paradigm that mistakenly affirms daily the idea that the 'primary reality' in life is the material world around us. It also convinces many of us that we ourselves are only three-dimensional material beings. Even our consciousness is frequently attributed to matter and a random consequence of brain chemistry.

Yet it seems more of us are now beginning to acknowledge a different and truer reality. We have seen in the last two decades a growing interest in the invisible, non-material dimensions of emotional and spiritual intelligence. Such topics are now perceived to be a vital part of management, leadership and even parental development. The recent expansion of interest: in mindfulness for individuals and within organisations; in EQ and SQ capabilities such as empathy and compassion, meaning making and values alignment; in the recognition that our state of being shapes what and how we 'do' what we do; in the necessity of leadership competences such as 'detached involvement' and reflective self-inquiry, are just a few of the many signs that an increasing number of organizations and their leaders are integrating a more non-material, some would say spiritual, approach to how we work together.

However, these are not academic subjects that can be left to the 'apparent' authorities on self-development and personal growth. In most academic arenas there is often a narrow understanding of the nature of consciousness, alongside agendas shaped by the pressures of the commercial and competitive world of 'doing', paying little attention to the primary shaper of all our actions, which is our state of 'being'.

The underlying premise of this book is that self-development is not only unnecessary, it is impossible. This is counter to almost the entire personal development industry. So this book is also a short course in 'undevelopment', appropriate for anyone interested in liberating their true nature and realizing their potential to live their life to the full.

Each of us carries an innate wisdom within our hearts. Not the heart of our body but the heart of our being. At the end of each chapter there are questions, contemplations and reflections that invite you to access that wisdom within your self. If you don't, then, in my experience, little will change for the better and you will likely add more layers of illusion and create more beliefs that will likely further suppress your own truths. So, I invite you push the Awareness Pause button, metaphorically speaking, and explore not only the information in each chapter, but just as importantly, the invitations to self-enquiry that follow. I only draw the maps, you are the territory.

I'm fairly certain that what you find here will also raise many questions, so feel free to challenge, ask awkward questions, exercise your curiosity or simply give me a hard time, at mike@relax7.com.

I can't teach you what you already know, but perhaps I can help you to remember.

1

The Wisdom of
PERSONAL UNDEVELOPMENT

"To attain knowledge, add things every day.
To attain wisdom, remove things every day".

Lou Tzu

The Mistake of Learning and Learning Mistakes

It's impossible to develop your self, and personal growth is an absurd idea.

If this statement be true then ...Houston, we have a problem!

Most of us have grown up with the received and accepted wisdom that it's essential to pursue 'self-development' and cultivate our 'personal growth'. When we end our formal schooling we tend to position our personal development under 'further education'. We encounter somewhat clichéd sayings like 'you never stop learning' and 'life is a school' or 'learning is growing'. Many of us will allow our self to be led up a garden path defined by the belief that we have to 'unleash' our unlimited inner resources in order to realise our so-called 'full potential' through our 'continuous learning' and 'personal growth'.

As a result, in the last three decades a substantial 'personal growth and self-development' industry has sprouted and many a guru, teacher, coach and trainer have developed their apparently unique approach to the 'development' of the self and the 'growth' of the person.

But it seems it may all be built on a mistaken and inaccurate set of beliefs. Once you start to challenge such beliefs as 'education is learning' and 'learning is development' and the 'self should be continuously growing and developing' it all starts to unravel. But it's only when you become aware and clear about who and what 'the self' is that it then becomes obvious that neither can 'you' grow nor can you develop your 'self'. Nor do you need to.

There are three ways in which to liberate your self from the illusions of self-development and personal growth - unlearning, undeveloping and undoing. The outcome is the restoration of what is often referred to as your 'true nature', which is already and always present within you.

1 The UNLEARNING Imperative

First is the recognition that many commonly accepted and assimilated beliefs need to be 'unlearned'. Some examples.

EDUCATION is not what you are taught to believe it is

For years we sat in a classroom absorbing huge amounts of information. At the end of each year we sat an exam and we were tested not so much on what we learned but how well we remembered what we were told. There may have been aspects of the testing that acknowledged our creative ability to express what we remembered. Occasionally we were challenged to combine and reflect on the contents of our memory. But largely it was a memory test. And memorising is not the same as learning.

We are mostly now aware of this confusion between learning and memorising. Although there are pockets of change in approach and emphasis, there is still no revolution within most mainstream education systems that is attempting to restore the true meaning of learning.

TIME isn't what you learned it was

Each day most of us will live by three illusions about time. First, you better hurry up as we're running out of time. Second, if we do this quickly we can save time. Third, let's do it later when there will be more time. Have you ever seen time running out? Where did it go? What ran precisely? Have you ever saved time? If so, where is it now?

Has there ever been more time later? No, no and no! It's the illusion that the machine on our wrist or the clock on the wall is time itself that keeps us feeling pressured and rushed. But the clock is not time, it's just a measuring machine.

The time is always 'now'.

STRESS isn't coming from where you learned it originated

Have you ever reacted emotionally to someone one day and then been calm and cool with the same person or situation the next day, or vice versa? Yes of course. That just reminds you that your stress is not created by other people or events, but by your self. All of it! At all times. In all places. But so deeply has the belief that 'it's them and not me' taken root that this is not an easy truth for most to accept.

WORK is not designed to 'give you' what you learned it could, should or would

Do you expect to feel fulfilled at work? Did you learn that you 'have to' find a job that satisfies you? Ever noticed that they don't? They can't. That's not the job of a job! It's your job to empty your self into whatever work you do and only then can you be fulfilled! Yes it's a paradox. To feel fulfilled you need to empty your self. Not exactly an insight acquired in 5th grade. Or any grade. By the way, you, the self, can never be emptied.

MONEY is not the basis of what you learned would give you a sense of security

In reality, when you hold this extremely common belief you are guaranteed to make your self feel insecure. Almost the entire population of our world is trapped in this one illusion alone. To believe anything material, anything that is constantly changing, constantly coming and going, can be used as a basis of security and stability, sits at the foundation of almost every human activity and almost all human suffering. It's not a small mistake. But it's hugely popular!

Just a few of the beliefs we all learn to assimilate and then allow to run our lives from within our consciousness. Many more will become apparent as you explore various areas of your life in the following chapters. It's obviously more effective if you can spot them for your self. It's in such moments of 'noticing' that you may think or say, "Now

I see why I am not happy, not truly free and quite unaware of reality". When you have such insightful moments, you reclaim a little more of your own power, you feel a little freer and you restore a little more clarity than you had a few moments before.

Unlearning is ultimately driven by the realization of the deeper truths that sit behind and beyond 'belief'. Beliefs obscure the truth. All the truths you need to realize are already there, within your consciousness, within you, awaiting rediscovery. But they are not static ideas. Truth is not an 'it'. It's not just another philosophy. It's not even possible to capture 'the truth' in words. Beliefs tend to be static but a 'truer awareness' and an awareness of what is true, arises and flows from particular states of consciousness. Cultivating that awareness is not something that can be taught beyond the theory of awareness itself.

Pure awareness only occurs when you are being your authentic self. Sounds easy but it's probably the hardest thing to do in our now busy and chaotic world where we mistakenly 'learn to believe' that we have to aspire and work hard to be someone or something other than our self.

2 The Mythology of Personal Development

Understanding why self-development and personal growth are myths becomes clearer when we see why and how such ideas and belief systems have put down such deep roots in so many cultures throughout the world? It's all to do with our understanding of what 'the self' is, and what the true nature of the self is.

It goes something like this.

The Necessity of UNDEVELOPING

There is one belief that permeates the consciousness of almost every human being. It's the belief that what you see in the mirror is what you are. It's prior to the obviously false 'money equals security' belief, and it sits at the 'core of the core' of all human unhappiness and suffering. It's a belief that is passed down from generation to generation and, as the old saying goes, it is the first sin visited by mothers and fathers upon their children. By 'sin' I just mean mistake. It's an innocent mistake that we all inherit. The reality is we are not what we see in any mirror. But it's best not to believe me!

Becoming aware of this mistake and then correcting it is the red thread that runs through almost all my books. Simply because it's so obviously the root cause of all our personal, interpersonal and international conflicts. It takes a little time to join the dots and fully realise how this mistaken belief lives in your consciousness and the effect it has had, and is having, on your daily life. So I describe this same mistake in different ways in different books simply because it tends to require repeated assimilation before the penny drops and you induce your own 'AHA, now I get it' moment. It's that moment when you transition from believing (others) to knowing (for yourself).

Undeveloping the World's Most Popular Illusion

There are two energies at play in the dance of life. Physical energy, which takes the solid form of material things like bodies. And spiritual energy, which remains formless but is referred to as consciousness or soul or spirit. Spiritual energy is primary and it animates form, giving the physical energy of our body its vitality. Spiritual energy is what you and I are. Sometimes referred to as 'the being' that is ...being!

These two energies are obviously highly integrated. Form cannot be alive without the life force of spirit/soul. And spirit/soul cannot create and express itself without occupying form. However, and here comes the big universal mistake, we do not consciously 'know' our self as spirit and we mostly 'learn to believe' our self to be form. Our sense of identity, our awareness of 'who I am', is built out of the idea that a solid, physical, material form is what 'I am'. We mistakenly develop what is known as 'body consciousness'.

How do you come to know you are spirit and not form? Only through your own insperience. Either through a moment when you realize that a material sense of self is an illusion OR through the elimination of all that is NOT the authentic you, and then noticing that what remains is 'the self', the being of consciousness. What remains is nothing that can be fully captured in a form-based language such as words and sentences. While many poets and philosophers, sages and gurus, have tried to describe the self as a spiritual being, they could only ever point or paint a word picture, not capture. Perhaps one of the best descriptions of self, in English at least, is 'pure awareness'.

Many people already 'believe' they are spirit, and therefore spiritual, but don't quite realise that it's not enough to just believe it and think it. It is necessary to know it and be it. But it cannot be taught, mentored, facilitated or coached in conventional ways, only indicated. The personal realisation of self as spiritual energy or pure awareness happens by what some have called 'grace' OR as the fruit of spiritual practices over a period of time OR by being in the presence of someone who is in a 'soul conscious' state.

Even then it's likely to be a temporary insight, a quick taste, metaphorically speaking, of what being soul/spirit feels like and is. One of the signs you have tasted your natural spiritual state is the realization that 'I am no one and no thing', I am just the 'I' that says, 'I am'. Except there is no thought of being the I, there is just a sense of what has been termed 'isness'. Just being.

As you bring this state of consciousness out into the world of thought, action and interaction, in the context of your relationships, you start to notice the 'nature of being'. You start to restore your awareness of your true nature. Once again words are inadequate to capture it, all they can do is provide a map.

The nature of every being is a peace that is not passive or submissive, but known and felt as an ever-present silence and stillness of being. Like the centre of a wheel around which everything revolves. It is love, but not in a narrow, romantic or subject/object exclusive sense, but an inclusive, all-encompassing, universal connection with everyone and everything sense. It is joyfulness, but not a happiness that is in any way dependent on any other person, circumstance or event. More a quiet, bubbling, inside-out kind of vitality that is often known and felt as the natural bliss that arises from an awareness of being a free spirit.

If red, green and blue are the primary colours found in physical nature, from which all other colours are made, then these three words, peace, love and joy, describe the primary states found in the true spiritual nature of every human being. All goodness is a combination of these three aspects of our being. It's a goodness that has no opposite, only degrees of deviation. When expressed in action this 'goodness' is sometimes referred to as virtue.

Neither your true state of being, as spirit/soul, nor the true nature of you, which has the capacity to be in a state of peacefulness, lovefulness or joyfulness, are developed. They are what each of us is, and can never be lost. We only distort them, obscure them and sabotage them, and thereby lose awareness of our trueness through all that we mistakenly develop. That starts from the first and original mistake i.e. the belief that we are only physical, material beings. All suffering and pain can be traced back to this single mistake. The correction of this mistake is ultimately the basis of all healing and 'self' revealing.

The Undevelopment of What?

How do you come to know your true, underlying, impossible to lose, most natural state of being? While you may realise your true underlying nature through some spiritual practices it's also necessary to 'undevelop' all that is false or untrue about you that you have developed within you. How do you know there is something that needs to be undeveloped? When there is suffering of any kind. Suffering is unnatural. Inevitable but unnatural. It's a signal there is something that needs to change within your consciousness just as sustained pain in the body is a signalling something needs to be healed within the body. Something that's been developed in consciousness in the past needs to be undeveloped in the present. Which brings us to the question, the undevelopment of what exactly?

Here are a few examples.

When you believe you are just a material form, you believe you are what your body looks like, so you 'develop' vanity and the fear that you may either never look good enough or lose your looks. You suffer.

When you believe you are just a material form, you believe YOU are not only decaying but that you will die. So you 'develop' the fear of death. More self-created suffering.

When you believe you are just a material form, you start to compare your form with other's forms and, as a result, 'develop' the habit of swinging between feelings of being beautiful or not so beautiful, superior or inferior. That's not being in your true peaceful nature. It's a form of suffering. Like all forms of suffering it's tolerable until it's not.

When you believe you are just a material form, your self-esteem i.e. your capacity to know your value, is obscured because you 'develop' the belief that your esteem should be based on material things such as looks or possessions or pay. All of which are changing in ways over which you have no control, so you 'develop' insecurity around your idea of your self. Causing not only more suffering but you are not an idea.

When you believe you are just a material form, you will likely 'develop' your sense of who you are out of what you do. You use your occupation to define your self so you develop anxiety around your position and perhaps your place in an organisation. Stress becomes inevitable.

When you believe you are just a material form, you 'develop' the belief that the objects you gather i.e. your possessions, actually belong to you, so you 'develop' the fear of loss or damage. We become possessed by our possessions and consequently develop a continuous free floating anxiety, which is suffering.

When you believe you are just a material form, you 'develop' a dependency on others for approval and acceptance of how you look and what you do, which you may then mistake for love. So when it doesn't come, you develop feelings of inadequacy and worry that you are not lovable and that such approval will not be forthcoming in the future. More suffering.

When you believe you are just a material form, you 'develop' and maintain the idea that you have needs. You develop worry/anxiety that your needs may not be met. Worry and anxiety are not exactly happiness. They are forms of suffering. By the way, while the body that you occupy has needs, you don't. But, once again, this is known only when you are being your authentic self!

The core belief that we are only a material form means we will inevitably 'develop' fear, insecurity, a loss of awareness of our value, anxiety, vanity, sadness and, well... the list becomes slightly endless. These misperceptions and resulting 'emotions' then become the basis for the development of the 'habits' that together, will shape our personality.

From fear (always of imagined loss) must come sadness (always following the belief something has been lost) from which comes anger.

We all tend to develop these emotional patterns to some extent or other. It just varies from person to person. But the common core reason is the same within all of us – the belief that 'I am' the height, shape, colour and progressively wrinkled form that I see in the mirror every morning.

This one core belief spawns so many other beliefs, which then cause many other forms of emotional suffering. From this one core belief grows what we call the 'material paradigm', which is a matrix of beliefs and values that we sustain in almost every culture of our world.

It's this 'I am just a physical form' mindset that also leads to the creation of a sense of hurt that is sometimes referred to as trauma. We all therefore contain memories of many traumas, some large and many small, which in turn interfere with our capacity to think calmly and act lovingly towards others. That's when we may need to engage in some therapeutic treatment for what appears to be a psychological problem. But it's really a spiritual issue otherwise known as a case of mistaken identity that's at the root for ALL psychological problems. But it's not so easy to make such a connection as it's just not part of our educational process to become so deeply and subtly self-aware.

No matter what the context is, all our suffering, all our unhappy moments, and all our inabilities to think and act with clarity and love towards others, can be traced back to the development of this mistaken belief around who I am.

That's why a significant amount of undeveloping would appear to be required if we are to be our self and know our true nature once again.

3 The End of the Growth and DEVELOPMENT Illusion

Everything in the material world grows. As it grows it develops. Plants and trees, birds and animals, insects and fish, all grow and develop physically.

When we learn to mistakenly believe that the self is simply a physical form, that you and I are essentially just bodies, we then take the idea of growth and development and apply it to our self. As we believe we are physical forms we then believe we grow and develop. So it's this belief that we are material entities that distracts from the truth that while our bodies do grow and develop we/you/I don't!

We do accumulate experiences and insperiences on our journey through life and living, but that's not growing, it's accumulating. You could say wisdom is the application of accumulated experience and is therefore 'developed'. But when you realise that all our experiences are filtered and interpreted through the beliefs and perceptions of self as 'material form' they become distorted and inaccurate interpretations, leading to a wisdom that is not grounded in truth. So it's not true wisdom.

While it's natural for the bodies and brains that we animate to grow, it's just not what happens within the being of consciousness that we are. But it's from this misunderstanding that the personal growth and self-development industry will arise and lead almost all of us astray.

In almost every area of human activity we encourage the development of experts and authorities. Our education systems are designed to produce such authorities. So once we accept the idea, the misbelief, that we are physical and therefore also develop, we find experts and authorities emerging in the areas of what becomes known as personal growth and self-development industry. Only fifty years ago, you would not have found many books and even fewer workshops on 'how to develop your self'. It's a relatively new concept. Not quite as new as the idea of 'self-esteem', but that's another seminar!

"Your physical body grows and develops but you don't!"

You can develop your skills and talents. That just takes mental and mechanical practice. They mostly fall into the mental/physical realm of action and doing. We'll return to the ideas of 'spiritual skills' and 'soft skills' shortly.

Notice that while our 'intention' and 'motivation' to develop skills and talents come from within our being, neither intention nor motivation are developed. They are always there, to some extent or other, naturally. But notice how they can fluctuate from day to day. Some days, in some situations, they are clear and strong and on other days not so clear and strong. Why? IT's because we learn to believe that we 'develop' our consciousness by absorbing the beliefs of others and accumulating many experiences. What we don't notice is that it's those learned and recorded beliefs and experiences within our consciousness that are the cause of our fluctuating intentions and motivation. They get 'in the way' and distract our attention and therefore distort and diminish the energy and enthusiasm of the self.

Once your consciousness is fully undeveloped, in other words freed from all illusion and misbelief, liberated from all attachment to the memories (experiences) you have learned to value and carry, your intention and motivation no longer lose focus or fluctuate. What was in the way is then out of the way!

You obviously don't want to deliberately undevelop a talent or a skill that you have already developed. That would not make sense. It would be a waste of time and energy considering the time and energy you have likely put into cultivating it. But if you let a skill or talent atrophy by not using it, you may notice that 'you' are not diminished. You are no less for the loss of a talent or skill. You are still you. Which means YOU are not your (developed) skills and talents.

The Awareness of No Reason

Once you become aware of who you are as a spiritual being i.e. the energy of consciousness that animates physical form, you will also start to restore the 'awareness' of your true nature. 'Knowing' it is not the same as reading about it, which is why this text can only ever point you in a certain direction and give you a map of what you will likely find for your self, within your self.

It's likely you have already connected with and been in your true nature but you were unaware of it at the time. Have you ever felt deeply content within your self for no reason? It's because you ultimately don't need a reason to be happy. It's your natural state of being. Have you ever extended care for someone for no reason? It's because you don't need a reason to be loving, to be caring. It's your nature. Have you ever felt deeply and profoundly peaceful for no apparent reason? You don't need a reason to be at peace. It's your nature.

Every evening we return home after a busy day and we eventually sit down to relax and be at peace. It's natural. Every day we feel inclined to care for someone or something, not because we are attached to them, but because it's what we intuitively know is the natural thing to do.

Even the worst criminal will probably care for their mother for no other reason than 'she's my mum'. It's natural.

Your true nature as a human being is always present within your being. It can never be lost and no one can ever extract it. It's what we each learn to believe and do that obscures it. We simply lose our awareness of it and our capacity to be it. As we have seen the cause of that comes down to one mistaken belief from which all other mistaken beliefs will arise. The belief that you are simply a physical form. That gives rise to the other misbeliefs such as happiness is pleasure i.e. a physical stimulation that must come from outside in; that love can only be known and felt when it comes from another; that peace is only possible when you are exhausted by physical exercise.

So what's in the way of being our authentic self and knowing our true and natural self? What stops us from residing in our true nature? Only our conditioning, which is made up of our recorded (memorised) beliefs and perceptions. These 'records' sit at the heart of all our 'habits' of thought, feeling and action. While understanding how our habits are formed and how to unform them is extremely interesting, it is not the most effective way to liberate our self from the conditioning that ensures we will live an unnatural life. But before we look at the most profound and effective way of liberation, let's explore the how and what of habits anyway.

The Anatomy of a Habit

Most of us are aware that a habit is an automatic action or reaction in relation to who or what is around us. It's a recording in our consciousness that is 'activated' or triggered (not caused) by someone or some event, either in the world out there, or in the mental world in here. But what goes into a habit? What sits within the recordings in our own consciousness awaiting activation as we create our 'autopilot reactions'?

If you have a television you may be aware that the signal containing the picture and the sound comes in via what is known as a coaxial cable. If you were to cut the cable and look at a cross section you will find a series of layers. The outer layer is plastic, then there is a layer of metallic gauze, then a layer of very thin aluminium, then another layer of plastic and then running through the centre there is a copper wire.

It's almost the perfect metaphor for all that goes into the creation of a habit.

Imagine a habit is like a multi-layered cable. It is a set of recordings in your consciousness in which you have stored memories at each level. The outer layer is the recording of the physical behaviour known as your reaction, the next layer is the emotion that is shaping the behaviour, the next layer is the thought/s that triggers the emotion, the next layer is the perception or interpretation that shapes thoughts, and the final layer, at the centre, is the original recording that started the habits formation in the first place, a belief.

Imagine someone rushes into the room and shouts RATS! In a split second some people would jump up on their chair (behaviour) feeling scared (emotion) because the thought, "Argh! I hate rats", occurs in their mind, because they perceive rats to represent a threat (perception) because some time in the past they learned or assimilated the notion that rats are dirty little disease carrying killers (belief).

Some people, however, would not jump up and scream but remain calmly seated. They have no such recordings in their consciousness. They are 'unconditioned' in their relationship to rats!

At the core of all our habits is a belief. The deepest belief and the belief that gives rise to all other beliefs is you are simply a physical form. From that comes the beliefs that your security is materially based, your happiness is a physical stimulation, that love requires a physical contact, that peace only occurs in quiet physical spaces, that joy is receiving a physical object etc. etc. So many beliefs and therefore so many habits. All together they create a cloak around our heart. Not the physical heart, but the heart of our consciousness where we will always find our true unconditioned nature.

The Great UNDOING

It would appear that taking away the cloak by 'undeveloping' all those habits, based on all those beliefs that are not true, would be the way home to your heart. It appears that the way back to being your true self and residing in your true nature would be to undo each and every habit based on a false belief. And you can do that, but it may take a little time! Sometimes it's called therapy. If you were to decide to do that, then what follows is an indication of what you may need to do within your consciousness.

If you want to be in your natural peaceful state you will need to undo the habit of anger (irritation, frustration, resentment).

If you want to be in your natural loving state you will need to undo the habit of fear (anxiety, tension, worry, panic)

If you want to be naturally contented you will need to undo the habit of judging others

If you want to be a free spirit you will need to undo the habit of attachment

If you want to restore a consistent clarity you will need to undo the habit of becoming emotional

If you want to feel and know the strength that lies in humility you will need to undo the habit of creating the ego

If you want to become enlightened you will need to undo the habits of endarkening your self

If you want to be naturally joyful (again) you will need to undo both the habits of excitement and sorrow

If you want to be empathic you will need to undo the habits of apathy and sympathy

If you want to be fully present you will need to undo the habit of drifting off into mental stories of past and future

If you want to be relaxed you will need to undo the habit of creating stress

If you want to be focused you will need to
undo the habit of over-thinking

If you want to be successful you will need to
undo the habit of allowing your intellect to become lazy

If you want to be spiritual you will need to
undo the habit of considering your self to be physical.

If you want to be authentic you will need to undo
the habit of building your identity out of what you are not

If you want to be respectful you will need to
undo the habits of criticizing and rejecting

If you want to be trusting you will need to
undo the habit of believing you've been offended

If you want to be forgiving you will need to
undo the habit of blame

If you want to know reality you will need to
undo the habit of deluding your self

If you want to forgive AND forget you will need to
undo the habit of believing others can hurt your non-physical feelings

If you want to 'know' you will need to
undo the habit of settling for belief

Sounds a lot like hard work, doesn't it? Besides, to attribute the
recovery of different aspects of your true nature by removing just one or
two habits is somewhat simplistic. All our habits are interconnected, all
our recordings are interwoven by a set of beliefs that are all interrelated.

That's why there are such spiritual practices that can take you directly back to your heart, back to your true nature. The most common of which is some form of meditation. It's 'on the way' back that you will notice which habits and their core beliefs are mostly 'in the way' for you personally. It's on the way back that you will have your insightful, realisations, your AHA! moments, as you realize the truths that are always awaiting your rediscovery. AHA – so happiness is not temporary pleasure, AHA – so my security is not dependent on money, AHA – so love does not have to be acquired from another for it is what I am, AHA – so I am responsible for all that I think and feel, for my own life, etc.

In your initial practice of meditation, and in your contemplations that follow, you will probably have short and powerful moments of being in your true nature. Gradually, such moments increase, and all those 'illusion based habits' lose their power to shape your thoughts and decisions.

When, one day, you are able to reside in your true nature for longer periods, you will start to notice you don't need to learn any new skills or abilities as you naturally find your true nature responding and expressing in true and natural ways.

Compassion, empathy, respect, caring, forgiveness, listening from the heart, nurturing, trusting, are often positioned as spiritual skills or soft skills. This implies they can be learned and developed. So off we go to the seminar or the workshop to be taught and even trained to develop such skills. But you can't 'learn' them. If you try it's unlikely they will be authentic. It's as if you will try to manufacture them for a reason! And you may well be good at doing that. But they will never feel quite right, quite true, quite real. There is always likely to be a feeling you are 'forcing' it, perhaps faking it.

But you don't need to learn such skills, which aren't really skills, as they will arise naturally when you are in your true nature, when you are being your authentic self.

Notice how empathy and compassion, caring and forgiveness, encouragement and nurturing, are all aspects of love in action. When you are being in your true nature, which is what we call love (not Hollywood love), then such abilities and capacities occur naturally in response to people and situations around you. As naturally as grass grows out of soil or fish swim in the ocean or ants share the load of community building.

Yes, you can practice trying to be caring and trying to be forgiving and trying to compassionate but, if you do, you are likely to notice you are not being completely genuine in your intention. The attempt to 'force the ability' is coming from a belief that you 'should be' more caring or forgiving, you 'should be' more nurturing and encouraging etc. So they are belief driven. Sometimes it's called idealism! Whereas, when you have restored your awareness of your true nature they come naturally and easily. Can you sense the difference? If they don't come easily and you do feel you have to force the ideal and try to train your self to be ideally caring and ideally forgiving, ideally nurturing, ideally encouraging, then it means there are still some old habits, some old beliefs, that are still 'in the way' of you being ...you! That's not bad or good. It just is.

So 'undeveloping' can take the form of 'undoing' all those habits of thought and action by 'unlearning' the beliefs that sit at their core. Or you can go straight to the heart of the matter and rediscover your authentic self and your true nature, at the heart of your being.

Many people combine both. A little therapy in order to realize and unravel the illusions that have been assimilated while disempowering the memories such illusions have created AND a little meditation, often referred to as the journey of no distance one second, and thereby inducing moments of self-realisation or the realization of the true self. This is the realisation of the inner space within each of us that is beyond belief, beyond idealism, beyond the urge or need to force anything.

And finally, what might be the other signs your true nature has been restored and you are being your true, authentic, easy, natural, powerful, free, unconditioned and 'undeveloped' self again?

1   You are aware that you are no one and no thing, but that you are amongst people who still believe they need to be someone.
2   You recognise that you play many roles in your life but you don't build your identity out of the roles you create and play.
3   You no longer identify with anything that is not you in either the material world around you or in the mental world within.

4   You are aware that you live in and through the material body that you occupy and that IT is not YOU.

5   Other than meeting the material needs of your body, you have no material desires as you no longer need anything physical to make you happy, as you have dissolved the misbelief that pleasure is the only happiness. That's not to say you do not enjoy and appreciate the pleasures that life brings you. Tricky, isn't it!

6   YOU have no personal needs other than the need to give of your self, which happens naturally when you are 'in your true nature'. It is therefore not a true 'need', but you are aware there is an imperative to meet the needs of your body.

7   No event in the material world around you shocks or surprises you as you recognise everything is unfolding both in the natural world and the world of human affairs exactly as it is meant to unfold.

8   You are not attached to anyone or any thing but you recognise every thing comes for use and everyone around you is a relationship that provides the opportunity to give and receive love, to be creative, co-creative and to discover your own ever deepening wisdom.

9   As there is no longer any attachment, you have ceased creating any emotional disturbances within your consciousness so that your feelings are consistently calm, clean and clear – always warm, yet cool!

10   You are able to naturally accept everything and everyone as they are, regardless of their history or their intentions.

11   There is no longer any suffering i.e. sorrow, unhappiness or stress, of any kind.

12   You recognise life is playful and you can be playful in all relationships and situations. Even the suffering of others is part of the playfulness of life and in your recognition of their suffering, love as compassion emerges naturally.

13   You are aware that the deepest cause of the suffering of others is always that sense of separation from their true nature.

Just as you 'once' were!

II

AWARENESS
PAUSE

Questions

What are the HABITS that you've developed that you know are:

a) wasting your time

b) stopping you from being more decisive

c) in the way of your ability to be calmer and clearer

Reflection

Recall moments when you felt peaceful for no reason and cared
for another for no reason.

Action

Research five different approaches for meditation.

Contemplation

> "Wisdom tends to grow in proportion
> to the awareness of one's ignorance."
> Anthony De Mello

2

The Wisdom of
TIME and STRESS
MANAGEMENT

> "Yesterday is gone. Tomorrow has not yet come.
> We have only today. Let us begin."
> Mother Teresa

Time never runs out and stress is completely curable!

It seems time management and stress management are the most highly attended courses/workshops/seminars in the world. Yet both time and stress management are oxymorons. 'Manage' implies control and the one thing you can never control is time passing.

And who 'manages' stress? When you're stressed it means you're not managing anything! The stress is managing you! Why would you want to learn stress management? Surely you want to be stress free. Unless of course you are still holding on to that popular illusion that some stress is healthy. Healthy stress? Another oxymoron?

Could it be that there are only a few among us who can see that you can't control the passing of time and you can't 'manage' stress? All you can control are your thoughts, feelings and actions 'in time' and about time, so that you no longer create stress. Perhaps that's why time management and stress management are code for self-management.

Measuring Change

We define time by the changing world around us. The clock is not time, it's just a machine. Clock time is the way we attempt to *measure our experience of the space between two events* either 'out there' in the world, or 'in here' within our consciousness. So if we cannot manage (control) time, which we can't, we try to control events. Most events involve other people so we try to control other people. The two things in life you cannot control are other people and events (more than three feet away from you!) It's therefore no wonder we make our self so stressed. We are trying to do the impossible, which guarantees our failure, which quietly kills our self-confidence. Certainly not a wise way to live.

When you try to do what you can never do i.e. try to control what you cannot control, most people create the emotion of frustration. Which resides in the emotional family of anger. This is the main reason there is so much anger in the world. The vast majority of us assimilate two fatal beliefs a) the world should dance to 'my tune' and b) the world should make me happy. Life just doesn't happen that way.

All you can do is control your response to people and events. So time management is really response management. Unfortunately, most of our responses are automatic. They are habitual creations, which means we are not fully conscious of what we think and do. We're asleep! So, if you want to become conscious and change your habitual reactions, including the habit of making your self frustrated and angry, it pays to awaken and 'undo' the habit, as we saw in the last chapter.

Waking up is at the heart of undevelopment. While this book won't 'make' you awaken or 'make' you wiser, it will indicate where and how to look within and see for your self. It will 'map out' the wisdom you may discover there. There is no escaping the fact that it's only when you realize your own wisdom will you then start revealing and restoring the true, powerful, liberated, enthusiastic, loving all the time, happy everywhere, self.

Are YOU Having the Time of Your Life?

It all comes down to one insight. Time management is, in reality, 'attention' management. Anyone attending a time management seminar is really asking, "How do I decide what to give my attention to first and for how long?" Which is code for, "What is most important to me"?

That's when we leave the world of tools, techniques and methods and enter the dimension of consciousness asking one question, "What influences my decisions about what to attend to at any given moment of my life?" The answer is always 'personal' i.e. only you know what it is for you. Ultimately you have to decide. Only you make up your own mind. Otherwise we would all be clones.

When you accept complete and full responsibility for the priorities in your life you will become very aware of the many internal influences upon your attention. Such as your beliefs, perceptions, values, attachments, goals, desires and relationships. In other words, almost all of life, inside and out, has the potential to influence what you give your attention to. This is what makes time management attention management.

No two people have the same inner and outer influences upon their attention. No one can tell you what your beliefs and perceptions are, or should be. Though many will try! You may even expect them to. No one can ever know your values or tell you what you should value. Though many may try. And no one can control what you become attached to. Though many do try, probably every day of your life.

Another reason people go on time management courses is they have already allowed themselves to be told what to give their attention to. They have allowed others to influence their priorities. But there are times, perhaps many times, when it doesn't feel right on the inside. In other words, what they have been told, what they have learned, does not sit easily in their heart or their head.

Shifting Attention

When you change your beliefs you will use your attention differently. When you consciously activate your values you will attend to people and activities differently. When you are no longer attached to something or someone you will no longer want to attend to them so much. When you have clear goals you will focus your attention differently than if you didn't. And when you want to be with someone you perceive as special it's likely your attention will be drawn to that person ...a lot. You can usually forget time or attention management if you believe you have fallen in love!

Where your attention goes your time flows. Time is attention. You are your attention. So you are time! There are no 'outside in' techniques or tools to manage your attention. It has to come from inside out, from the heart of you. But that's unlikely to happen for most people for the following reason. See if you recognize it within your self.

Most people go on time management courses because they are not enjoying what they are doing. There is little or no joyfulness in their life. This is usually because they have been taught to believe that the job they do should 'give' them joy, or at least satisfaction. And maybe in the first few days or weeks it seemed so. But it can't, obviously. Life works the other way round. We are designed to bring our joy from inside out and therefore put it into all we think and do. In attending the time management seminar we are really saying 'please tell me or show me how to live my life', which is code for 'please show me how to enjoy my life', which is code for 'tell me how to find joy in life'.

Creative Consciousness

Someone who experiences 'inside out' joy while they do what they do is oblivious to the passing of time. They are beyond time management philosophies and techniques. It's irrelevant to them. Their joy brings forth their creativity and their creativity brings forth their joy, which then infuses their work and their relationships with enthusiasm. This in turn brings further joy.

Whenever you become 'time conscious' i.e. start watching the clock, it usually means you want to be somewhere else. You would rather not be where you are. Why? You are not finding any joy as you do what you are doing. Reason? You're not meant to.

Creativity is the key. When you are being creative notice how you lose all awareness of the passing of time. When you are being creative the joy you feel doesn't arise momentarily at the end of the process with some external 'achievement'. Joy occurs throughout the whole creative process of whatever you are creating. It's an internally created insperience! But if we expect to receive joy from the job, or from the people we work with, or from the circumstances, we will always eventually be disappointed and eventually bored. The disappointment then becomes habitual, morphing into reluctance and resentment, which then grows into a perception of ones inability to cope with the work, which then has us seeking some help in the form of a training to manage our time and our stressbetter.

Common Ingredients

It's no accident the two most common ingredients across all time management courses are prioritization and goal setting. When you are not enjoying life then it's almost impossible to prioritize i.e. make clear decisions about what is most important to you and therefore what should get your attention. And when you are not happy what's the point of setting goals when they are likely to prolong the misery.

What we seldom notice, sitting behind our capacity to prioritize and set our self some clear goals, are our values. But values are personal. As soon as your life is aligned to 'your' values then those who would want to make your choices for you will lose their influence over you. Hence the industries of advertising and marketing, along with many businesses, would prefer you to live according to the beliefs and values they will give you and not the values inherent in your own being. Unfortunately, we allow our self to be influenced by their messages and over time have our beliefs and values shaped for us. And we won't even notice.

Do you know how to value?

Values are what you have decided you care about the most. Yet values are not objects. To 'value' is something you are born to do. In its truest meaning, 'value' is not a noun, it's a verb. The ability to ascribe value is built into your consciousness. Both your ability to ascribe value and what you decide to care about cannot be imposed by others. Only you get to decide what you care about and only you get to choose whether or not to refresh that 'caring', that valuing, every moment of every day of your life.

Caring (valuing) is like a spiritual muscle. If you allow others to tell you what to care about, if you confuse caring with worrying, if you stop caring for any reason, it's as if you stop using your primary spiritual muscle. It's similar to not using some of the muscles in your body. Over time they just waste away and you will find it hard to recover your strength. Then you need others to help you up, to help you walk, to help you on and off cars and boats and planes.

Most of us have allowed our spiritual muscles to atrophy and the primary sign is when someone asks us what our values are and we say something like, "I'm not sure". Which is the same as, "I don't know". Or we just repeat what we have been told to value. Which is often what we have become attached to. Valuing is not attaching!

When we don't know what our values are it's often a sign we don't really know 'how to value' and we are not aware that that's what we are designed to do. 'Valuing' is where many of our feelings of satisfaction and meaning come from. And if we are no longer creating our own satisfaction and meaning for our self we allow others to do it for us. Laziness sets in. So we become susceptible to advertising, dependent on political propaganda, parental propaganda, cultural propaganda to provide us with 'shots' of apparent significance and meaning.

Notice when you care about something or someone you have no hesitation in giving them your attention and therefore your time. The last thought in your mind while intending to care and behaving in caring ways is 'I need to learn to manage my time better'. You may also notice that when authentically caring for anyone or anything there arises a feeling of satisfaction and contentment, if not a quiet joy, from inside out. That's why such 'valuing' moments are filled with meaning and significance.

So if there is a 'step one' in the universe of personal undevelopment it's the restoration of your ability to consciously manage your attention. It's undoing the habit of believing what your values should be, just because that's what you were told, and consciously deciding what/who you value i.e. what you care about or who you care about, by making a list of such values. Then consciously moving your attention in those directions. But you won't be able to do that until you stop allowing your attention to be distracted and drawn to what matters little to you.

That's why it's almost essential to start unlearning and undoing the habits of giving your attention to the superficial, to the gossip, to the easy sources of stimulation, to the keyboard and screen, to where you may acquire a short term reward of stimulation. Until those habits are gone they will distract you and pull your attention. They will push towards wasting your time and therefore your attention.

Once again, be careful you don't get your values mixed up with your attachments. They are not the same. Most people say they care about their car, or their house, or their partner, but they really mean, 'I am attached'. Attachment brings worry and sorrow. Caring brings forth only love. Take a few moments to reflect on the difference between caring and attaching. It's not what they taught us in school. But it will help you understand why billions of us make our self unhappy, unsatisfied and discontented, every day.

More about attachment later

Prioritizing your Values

Once you've decided what or who you care about it's time to ask your self which ones you care about more than others. This general prioritizing of what you are going to value then influences your general life decisions about what you will give your attention/time to. Then, in each of the areas or relationships that you have decided you value, you can set a goal. But then again you don't have to. It's not compulsory. You won't fail at life if you don't. Though some would say you will. What do you think?

The argument for not setting goals is that being 'goal oriented' means you are always focused on the future achievement of the target or the aim, for your self. You are therefore often never fully present as you are thinking too much about the forthcoming achievement. And if you are not present you are absent from your own life. Then it will be impossible to bring the joy of your own heart to your life moment by moment.

Then there is the constant struggling and striving for the goal. Often driven by the fear of failure. Are you goal driven and therefore fear driven? If you are aiming at a goal for the benefit of others it's often so that you can gain their approval and applause. Not always, but often. That generates anxiety. That's just more stress. Do you need others approval and applause?

The final argument against goal setting is if you are not honest then you may not notice the reason you want to reach the goal is because you 'believe' only then can you be happy. That's not right or wrong, but you are making your happiness dependent on some external achievement in one particular moment in time, in the future. No problem if you are, but is that where authentic happiness comes from? Is that how you sustain your happiness? You will obviously be the one to decide.

More about happiness later.

Decision Making

The case FOR setting goals in the areas of your values is that it helps you decide the use of your energy, which means your attention, which means your time. Many, without such a focus, find themselves in a kind of mental chaos, which is filled with worries such as, "Oh dear, I'm sure I'm wasting my time and therefore my life on this" or "Everyone else seems so clear about what they want to achieve, there must be something wrong with me" or "I feel so guilty not paying attention to them".

But you will have to decide for your self whether this is true or not for you. Do 'enlightened souls' have no goals? Some say they do! Do they live from moment to moment simply meeting and consciously responding to everything and everyone that comes in front of them? Some say that's all they need to do. Does this enable them to live with greater love, with real care, in all its various forms, making them more influential in the context of their work and relationships? Many say it does? What say you?

They even indicate that this goalless yet valuing approach to life generates deeper feelings of fulfillment and satisfaction. They are fulfilled because they are exercising their creativity according to the context or situation they are in. And they are satisfied through the 'giving' of their energy unconditionally to others. It's almost the opposite of what we are taught or programmed to do, which is not to give, but to get, acquire, accumulate and keep as much as we can. Such are the aims of our formal education and our cultural influences in a competitive material world.

The Creativity Route

A more enlightened way of living might look like the following. You take time out to identify what your talents and attributes are. You fine-tune your list to discern your most creative. You seek ways and means (creatively) to find the kind of work that allows you to use your creativity.

Creativity is not just about painting, poetry and music, it's about how you create your relationships and ultimately your life, which, in the context of earning money to live, can range from setting up a business, carving out a career path, discovering a vocation to doing charitable work.

The job/vocation you choose may require working in a 'position', working for someone else, or as a freelance, or just producing things you know other people would value. What you do to earn your crust is usually best directly linked to your creativity. This allows you to bring your joy to work but also bring it to all other areas of your life. Then time management will never be a necessary item on your things to learn list. It's the unenlightened soul (having perhaps not yet discovered their creativity) that buys into all they have been taught about work, productivity and goals etc. They often develop the mindset of what is often referred to as a wage slave - dependent on the income from a place that demands their labour in a structured and organized way.

Their dependence on doing something they don't particularly want to do for a living means they are perpetually unhappy and probably insecure, while convincing themselves this is the way to happiness and security. They will likely create feelings of being under pressure. At some point they may think or say, "I can't handle the pressure, I need some help to manage my time better".

The middle path is the person who goes to their current position at work but does what they do creatively. They make themselves of value to others wherever they are. They respond proactively to every situation and relationship. This attitude then naturally attracts other opportunities as new doors open. Confidence grows. Any debilitating habits of resistance, reluctance and resentment towards work or colleagues in the workplace start to atrophy naturally.

Liberation from Stress

One of the most popular stressors is the clock. We use the clock to create the perception and feelings of 'time pressure'. Although it appears that it's the time that is creating the pressure, it's not. It never is. The clock is just a machine that we invented to attempt to measure our experience of the space between two events. Any pressure we feel is never 'clock created' it's always self-created.

Many of us will think or say 'I am so stressed' and then blame the job or the boss or the amount they have to do or the threat of redundancy or the lack of money or the lack of time or the weather. It can be an endless 'list of blame'.

But it's obviously none of those things. It never was and never is. This is so hard for many of us to see. We have all been so deeply conditioned to believe our stress comes from outside in. We have also been conditioned to believe that a bit of stress is natural and can be healthy. This truly is to be fast asleep.

All moments of stress are moments of suffering such as sorrow, sadness, fear or anger. Otherwise known as unhappiness. Any moment of mental or emotional suffering is a messenger that comes to tell us there is something 'I need to change'. But we don't acknowledge the messenger very often, until perhaps it's too late, simply because we believe stressful feelings, unhappy feelings, come with the package called life on earth! We have learned to believe that stress is inevitable as well as natural! So there is no need to do anything about it. More sleepiness.

Even when we realize it's me that has to change, not them, most of us still shoot the messenger preferring the laziness of blame to the effortful changes we may need to make to our perceptions, thoughts and feelings. Realizing our self-responsibility means we also realize it's time to undo our habit of making our self suffer. Avoiding this level of inner work is a habit in itself.

So let's cut to the chase. You don't need to manage stress. Who would want to do that anyway? It's time to liberate your self from the habit of making your self unhappy. But you will only do that for your self when you fully *realize* and *integrate* each of the following insights into your day-to-day life.

1 You are 100% responsible for your emotions and feelings at all times and in all places. That means you create all your own stress.

2 You cannot control other people. Even when they seem to do what you want 'they' still make the decision to do what they do, or not do. Including children!

3 Happiness is an inside job. It is NOT pleasure. Pleasure and happiness are two different feelings. Pleasure derives from some physical stimulation, which may lead to dependency. Happiness arises from the heart of your being when you think and act in alignment with your intrinsic (true) nature.

4 You are never a victim. Your body may be, but 'you' are not, ever! It's an illusion to believe you are. But we identify our self with 'victim' when we believe we are only a physical form and that all our feelings are physical.

5 Your true nature is to be loving, joyful and contented. But this is not to be believed, it is to be realized for oneself, otherwise it's just an idea. Rediscovering your true nature is like restoring the vitality of your being. However, there are many old assimilated beliefs, perceptions and memories that are in the way. These are the basis of the many habits that require unlearning, undoing and undeveloping.

6 You create your life only when you are the master of the 'faculties of your consciousness'. This is self-mastery. More about your 'faculties' later.

7 Adversity is your greatest teacher until it teaches you there is, ultimately, no such thing as adversity.

8 There is no such thing as healthy stress or positive stress or necessary stress. Many just accept the beliefs that there is because they heard it somewhere.   Often because it's easier to believe than to do the work of taking responsibility those habits! Stress is a sign you need to adjust your perceptions which usually means unlearn some belief/s or other.

9 All stress arises from the ego. This is why the ego is the cause of all suffering.   (Not pain - pain is physical and suffering is mental/emotional). When you stop creating an ego you will liberate your self from all stress i.e. mental/emotional suffering. More about the ego later.

10 You have realized no one ever hurts your feelings. You do that. Once realized, you can never be offended!

Yes, you're probably right in thinking that this is the description of a saint. But you have to start somewhere! As the old saying goes, 'in every saint there was a sinner and in every sinner there is a saint'

Relaxing into Spaces of Time

We live in time **and** space but we seem to have less time **in** space and it appears we are finding it harder to create spaces of time!

As the world around us moves faster there is an increasing feeling that there is less time available. That's because we try to create and deal with more events in the same space of clock time today than we did yesterday. When more events require our attention, or we become addicted to being distracted by events, it feels as if life is speeding up.

Whether you are a teenager on your game console or an executive on the corporate ladder or a mother with attention seeking children or the overweight person seeking wisdom on the best foods to lose weight, it's not hard to create the perception of being under pressure. It's all magnified and turbocharged by the information age which provides instant access to the latest games, the latest corporate moves, the latest mothering techniques, the latest dietary advice, the latest movies etc., all streaming to a computer, smartphone or television near you.

According to some research it seems that we see and absorb more images in one day than people did in one year only 100 years ago. Intense 'time consumption' is code for intense 'information processing' which then generates the perception and feeling of a 'time famine'. We then allow the empty, quiet and reflective spaces that used to punctuate our lives to be squeezed out as we increasingly surrender our attention to ever more varied sources of electronic stimulation.

This shrinking of time and space is most visibly seen and invisibly felt when we act and interact with others. As we feel the pressure to act faster, action becomes reaction and reaction becomes habit. How often have you created an awkward situation or a relationship that requires repair because you hurriedly let the words just tumble uncontrollably out of your mouth or an emotion to instantly erupt?

Patience and presence, the signs and signals to the other that we care about them, disappear i.e. the patience to listen deeply to the other and our total presence to be with the other.

Whenever we 'react' instead of 'respond' it means we have 'collapsed' the natural space in our consciousness between receiving/perceiving the event and our action in response. To react is to allow conditioned habits to take us over and shape our thoughts, feelings and actions. When this happens it's usually a combination of *laziness* and a lack of *awareness*.

It is *lazy* because it's easier to react than create a patient and considered response. But the price we pay is often the guilt and regret that accompany such thoughts as, "I can't believe I just said that, it just came out that way, I couldn't help my self". Over time, as our reactive habits become deeper, the state of our relationships may reflect our lack of thoughtful consideration, and even our physical health may reflect the unruly negativity that is often buried in our reactive patterns.

It all points towards a loss of the *awareness* of our 'inner space'. We have lost our natural capacity to create a 'space of time' between the event and our response. It's only when we are fully present in this inner space that we are able to bring the eye of our intellect to calmly see the scene or situation with clarity. Then we can hear our natural wisdom (intuition), discern the most appropriate response, and creatively manifest it in our behaviour.

Our 'reactions', as opposed to responses, to anyone or anything seem to happen automatically. All 'reactivity' is emotionally driven, even though the flaring of emotion may be short lived. In such moments it's as if the emotion is in control of the self. If we allow such reactive tendencies to grow it feels as if our life is out of control.

Whether it's the occasional isolated incident, or a daily pattern, one solution is to interrupt the reactive patterns and relearn how to create 'space of time' between the event and the reaction, between stimulus and response. This can seem challenging, even difficult, at first. It feels like we are going against the very grain of our programming. And we usually are.

Here are some 'easy start' possibilities that may help you create a gap between life as it arrives to you and how you choose to deal with it.

Ten Ways to Create and Relax into Spaces of Time

1 Counting to 10 Before Responding

This is an old, favourite with many, method to create space between the event and your response. You may only need to reach 6, and when you do you know you have effectively pushed your inner pause button.

2 Deep Breathing

Try taking a complete breath cycle, slowly (in and out), before you speak, or two complete cycles, or four cycles. It not only becomes a good habit but you will notice how relaxed your body becomes and how much calmer your mind 'can' be.

3 Thought Stopping

Not so easy but nevertheless effective. Imagine a train travelling between stations slowing down and then stopping half way. So allow your 'train of thought' to do the same. You are not stuck, just waiting for the signals to change. In the meantime you have time to 'consider'. And then slowly move forward again.

4 Be Humorous

Find something in what the other has said or done that is light and humorous and focus on that before you respond. It softens your perception and interrupts any sharp emotions.

5 Visualize Creatively

If you have a 'challenge' with one particular person take a few moments before you meet them and visualize them in a positive light. Surround them with good wishes in your mind. Then, if things get sticky when you encounter them in reality, and you feel a 'reaction' arising, recall the visualization

6 Sip Water

Stuck in a meeting? Are you becoming increasingly reactive as the meeting wears on? Start waiting until 'after' you have reached out, picked up your glass, and sipped some water, before you respond. And if someone takes your airtime away then let them. It gives you more time to reflect and consider. You might be surprised how often you realize that what you were going to say isn't that important.

7 Request Repetition

Always a good way to buy some time in the meeting. Just say, "I didn't quite get that, could you run it past me again please". You did get it, but now you have some space to coolly craft your response.

8 Affirm a Delay

You could actually say to the other, "I'd like to think about this for a few moments, or a few hours, or a few weeks"! And give your self a big space.

9 Be Honest

There is nothing to beat being honest. Instead of letting the emotion translate into words and an emotive reaction, you could just say, "Look, right now I am feeling a bit reactive, my emotions are running high around this issue and getting the better of me. Can we come back to it later?" When you do this it means you are consciously facing and acknowledging your emotional state and that in itself will diminish the power of the emotion to hijack your thoughts and actions.

10 Meditate Frequently

If you are a practising meditator you will already know that you become much less reactive when you build moments of meditation into your day. Meditation itself is the creation of space, an inner space, which is beyond time. Meditation is the journey into your own inner timeless dimension, your consciousness. And once you master the practise you will find you are able to do it anywhere, anytime, but not lose your awareness of what is going on in the time driven world around you.

II
A W A R E N E S S
P A U S E

Questions

What aspects of how you use your time do you find
a) the most difficult and why?
b) the most easy and why?

Select three current situations or relationships where you
experience stress. Looking at each situation to what extent
do you take responsibility for your feelings on a scale of 1 to 10
where 1 is low (you don't) and 10 is high (you do).

Reflection

What are the ten most important things in your life?
Prioritize them. Then decide what you will 'do', perhaps change,
to affirm each ones 'relative' importance.

Action

Take a moment at the end of the day and write down all the
activities that received your attention today - even the smallest
actions for the smallest amount of clock time. Then look across
the list and mark each either:
V = valuable use of time
D = delegate next time
W = waste of time, don't do again
N = not the best time to do that

Contemplation

"It's not the load that breaks you down,
it's the way you carry it"
Lou Holtz

3

The Wisdom of
SELF MANAGEMENT

"Until you are the master and commander of
your consciousness most relationships
will be fraught with difficulty".
Anon

One big hole in all our educations

There was and still is a huge hole at the center of most of our formal
approaches to education. It's the one thing no one ever teaches us.
Otherwise known as 'self-understanding'. If you don't understand you,
you cannot manage you. If you cannot manage you i.e. the energies of
your thoughts, feelings, emotions and perceptions, then you will not be
able to manage, as well as you could, the four R's in your life - your
responsibilities, relationships, roles and resources.

The first principle of self-management is self-responsibility. It's the
realization that we are each 100% responsible for our thoughts and
feelings, at all times, in all circumstances. When we absorb and
empower the belief that other people and events shape our thoughts
and feelings we are, in effect, disempowering our self. We then see our
self as 'victim' and play the role of the victim, even if it's just for a few
moments and even if it's just to complain about the weather. In such
moments we are saying, "The weather is more powerful than me".
Physically that may be true but spiritually it is never true.

In fact, complaining, blaming or criticizing anyone or anything is a moment when we place our power, our destiny, in someone else's hands. It's not easy to see this clearly as we have all been brilliantly taught by two world class teachers that we are not responsible for our self or our circumstances. Those teachers are Hollywood and Bollywood (amongst others!)

In other words the media and entertainment industries! Almost everything they produce, every drama, every scene, every character, teaches us that we are at the mercy of circumstance, the victim of other people's behaviors, powerless in the face of events and other people's attitudes and actions.

While others may cause us physical pain, no one causes our mental or emotional suffering. That's why pain is compulsory and suffering is optional. It seems more and more people now 'get' this truth as they relearn how to be the master of their own consciousness. Pain happens to the body but not to 'the self'. The self creates suffering for itself. Until, that is, the self realizes the suffering is born of an illusion the self is creating about the self. Otherwise known as ego. More about the ego later.

Coming Home to Your Self

The foundation of our journey back to self-mastery is the cultivation of self-awareness. It's only an increased self-awareness that leads to a greater self-understanding that then results in self - management. It's that simple, in theory. But self-awareness itself is not that simple. In its truest sense self-awareness is not becoming more aware of the self, it's the self becoming more aware of what the self is creating within consciousness, which is the self!

"The simplest definition of meditation is the 'cultivation of self-awareness".

There are a number of methods to enhance self-awareness including reflective enquiry, contemplation and conversation.

There is now a huge industry built around many therapies and coaching practices in which we can allow someone else to help us become more self-aware. The oldest and most effective way to enhance your awareness of what is occurring within your consciousness is meditation.

It's in the meditative process that we begin to see the exact nature and quality of our creation in the forms of our perceptions, thoughts, emotions, attitudes and perspectives. These are not just random events in consciousness. Not knowing, not being aware, of both 'how or why' we create certain thoughts, emotions, attitudes and perceptions are popular forms of ignorance or ...unawareness.

It's in meditation that you see for your self the ways in which you sabotage your self. Only in the 'seeing' do you come to know what you need to undo within your self in order to be the authentic you again, and thereby restore the mastery of your consciousness. One outcome is you naturally stop creating any feelings of unhappiness regardless of what is happening around you. Both the process of becoming self-aware, and the 'AHA moments' along the way, are known as self-realization. Often referred to as 'awakening'.

If you ever decide to integrate self-awareness practices into your life, as a way of restoring your self-mastery, you 'may' see and realize the following for your self.

1 Who you are

Self-realization at the deepest level means realizing you are simply a conscious being. In effect you are consciousness itself. Some use other terms such as spirit, or soul, or the authentic self. They all refer to the 'I' that says 'I am'. Anything after 'I am' is not you. This awareness of the authentic self is also sometimes referred to as 'awareness' itself. This deep correction of one's sense of identity changes almost everything. Not only how you see your self, how you feel within your self, but also how you regard and interact with others.

2 What you are

With the on-going practice of meditation you may start to notice that your true underlying nature is a quiet peacefulness and a natural intention towards loving care. This peace is known by the silence and stillness that is always existing at the heart of your being. It's the non-moving, non-changing, aspect of your consciousness (which is you) that is always present and can never be lost. From this inner space of 'no place' arises the natural impulse to connect, which means to give, to love. Not Hollywood love, but the highest and purest emanation of consciousness itself.

3 How you work

With regular meditation you may start to notice the three main faculties of your own consciousness i.e. of your 'self'. You have a MIND for creating and giving form to your thoughts. You have an INTELLECT for evaluating and assessing the quality of your creation as well as discerning which thoughts should be translated into action and which thoughts need to be ignored or destroyed. Then you may see that your PERSONALITY is simply the accumulation of all your 'habits' of thought and action at the mental, emotional and physical levels.

You are not your brain. The brain is the hardware, the mind/intellect/personality is the software and YOU are the operator. But don't try convincing a scientist, or anyone who has 'scientific inclinations' of any of that, they probably won't 'get it'! They probably won't 'want' to get it. Besides, there is no need, once you see for your self.

4 Where you are

As meditation re-awakens the intellect and its clarity is restored you will start to see and know the 'context' of your life with that same clarity. You will notice each of us gets to create our life 'through' the form we occupy. As unique beings we create our own unique story. Our creation is authentic and powerful according to the extent to which we have realized we are never a victim of anyone or any circumstance.

While we get to create our personal journey, 'we' are all in it together. The quality of our relationships is the most significant part of our story. Our individual part in creating and sustaining those relationships is the primary factor contributing to our own happiness.

In the story of your life you can create and play as many roles as you wish. Indeed, everyone receives that same opportunity. But for most of us this is not clear. When we take life too seriously (because we forget who/what we are) we lose the 'creative playfulness' that allows us to switch easily from role to role in ways that are joyful, challenging and meaningful.

5 How the world works

With the regular practise of meditation comes insight and an understanding of the basic laws that govern the various levels of energy i.e. physical, mental and spiritual. At each level there are natural laws that exist to maintain harmony and balance. When we attempt to break any of those laws the result is always pain (in the case of physical laws) and suffering (in the case of mental and spiritual laws). These laws are not manufactured but 'built in' to each level.

Gradually with the on-going integration of meditation into daily life there arises many other insights and realizations that are fundamental to the cleaning and clarity of our awareness. These include our sense of purpose, our vision (an intuitive 'seeing') of how our life will unfold and the capacity to always create the wisest and most empowering responses in our interactions with others.

While there are many teachers of the above, when we try to learn about our self from 'outside in' it makes little difference to our life and the way we live. The absorption of more information does not fully awaken or nourish the soul/self/spirit that we each are.   It eventually has to come from 'inside out'.   It has to be self-realized. That happens when there is consistent integration of five practices into our daily life; meditation, contemplation, application, contribution and maintaining good company.

The self aware Self!

Many people have tried meditation and found it wasn't what they believed it was cracked up to be. Others had great expectations only to have their hopes dashed. While some dip in and out of practice, according to their inclinations and timetable. And then there are the 'dabblers' who are always on the lookout for new and better ways to 'do it', dabbling in various techniques as they go. All would probably consider themselves to be 'practising meditators'.

Meditation is as old as the Eastern hills and during the last two decades it's been occupying an increasing number of Western minds. But where do you start? Dip into the menu of 'types of meditation' and you will find a dizzying number of approaches, some ancient, some newly 'designed', some with recognized 'pedigrees' stemming from ancient origins, others appearing from nowhere in particular. Some are practised sitting down, some standing up, and some are done while 'strolling' around.

Then there are the promises. Some promise greater concentration, some guarantee deep relaxation and others dangle the carrot of enlightenment. Some should be done as the sole form of spiritual practice, some are just one of several practices necessary for the awakening and purification of the awareness that is the self. And some forms of meditation have become required practice within a religious vocation. Many approaches and 'methods' are free of charge so there is no commercial 'price comparisons' to assess the apparent efficacy of each. You cannot reliably consult a comparison website or blog review as everyone will have such different experiences of different approaches for a variety of obvious reasons.

So for all those new to the idea and practice of meditation it's no surprise they find it challenging just choosing where to start.

While one meaning of meditation is the cultivation of self-awareness, ultimately self-awareness is its own method, and whether you call it meditation or not, it is simply 'the self' becoming and being more aware of what is occurring within 'the self'! In essence, it is the self awakening, unfolding and revealing all that lies dormant, distorted and distracted within the self! It is the self seeing and freeing the its self from the blockages, barriers and boundaries both learned and assimilated on life's journey so far. And as it does, a form of inner integration and healing takes place. Hence many schools of meditation strongly associate healing with the origins and practice of meditation.

If you sit quietly for a few minutes you will probably discover that you cannot sit quietly for a few minutes! The noise of an addictively busy mind will distract and defeat your attempt to be at peace and to clearly see beyond the fog of your own thoughts and emotions. With practice your ability to sit quietly for a few minutes will expand, as will your awareness of what exactly is going on within your consciousness.

Meditation is essentially observing, noticing and allowing all that is happening within your awareness to just ...happen! The moment you notice and know that YOU are not what is 'happening' then you could be said to be on the 'edge of enlightenment'. You will also likely realize that while 'meditation' may have many formal forms with lineages and titles and labels and processes, the true process of meditation is an informal, unstructured, 'in the moment now' insperience of pure awareness. You may then also come to realize there can only ever be one 'kind' of meditation and that is 'your' meditation.

In the meantime, here are seven good reasons to get started.

Meditation as True Self Awareness

Few of us truly know who and what we are. We have learned to base our sense of identity on what we are not (body, position, place, possessions, labels etc.). Our awareness is then limited and defined by what we identify with. Meditation, along with contemplation are often seen as the only ways to see and release all our false identities, which we have allowed to take root deep within our consciousness.

Meditation allows you to rediscover your true consciousness as spirit or soul or, if you prefer, 'pure awareness'. This, in turn, sets you free from the feelings of insecurity that come when you base your sense of 'who I am' on something that is not your self.

With a little meditative practice you will even see that while your deepest beliefs 'appear' in your awareness they are also, in a sense, outside your 'self'. Beliefs are created, recorded and held by 'the self'. So you are not your beliefs. Like an archive in a university, the university is not the archive, but contains the archive.

Meditation as Right Thinking

The aim of meditation is not to stop thinking. Thoughts themselves can be a starting point for observing and witnessing. Practice watching your thoughts and ask 'who is the watcher, who is aware of these thoughts'. As you do you will notice the 'quality' of your thoughts.

Meditation will eventually help you to more consciously discern and control both the quality and direction of your thoughts. Not forcefully but naturally.

In this way, your mind ceases to harbor small thoughts of superficial things while the recovery of your true underlying nature will start to shape your thinking peacefully and lovingly i.e. in ways that reflect your true spiritual nature. Meditation reduces the 'quantity' of your thoughts and generates a higher 'quality' of thinking, which benefits you, your relationships and your work.

Meditation as Contemplation

Everything that happens in life has some meaning and significance. Unfortunately, we live so fast that we often miss the deeper meaning of events and the true significance of those people who pass through our lives. When you stop to 'contemplate' a specific situation or even just an object, you are using a meditative process to allow the event or object to trigger an awakening of meaning and significance within your consciousness. If you reflect and peacefully contemplate any scene at work today or on any current relationship, your consciousness will open like a flower to reveal insights and observations that can help you in such scenes and relationships in the future. If you find that hard to do it's usually because you are creating a judgment, which then triggers some form of emotional disturbance within your consciousness. That emotion has to be explored and resolved before clarity can be restored and insight induced. More about emotions later.

Meditation as Visualisation

We are all artists and our mind is our canvas. If you create a peaceful scene on the canvas of your mind, and meditate on that scene, i.e. allowing it to remain in your mind without becoming attached to it, investing it with depth and richness, you will begin to generate powerful feelings of peace and contentment from inside out. This replaces the dseire to be stimulated from outside in. At the other end of the spectrum, if you envision your goals, your preferred future outcomes, and if you don't become attached to them, then you will begin to attract towards you the necessary energies and circumstances to make them happen. Meditation helps you to concentrate and create – inner abilities that many of us have lost in our fast and frenetic media driven cultures. Once again, it's likely to be some kind of emotional disturbance that may get in the way of your capacity to concentrate and create with daily clarity.

Meditation as Silence

The most powerful place within your consciousness is at the core – it is the place of silence and stillness. It is this 'inner space' within each one of us that never changes. It is also your inner source of personal power – the power that you need to think and discern accurately. Meditation is a way into that inner silent space. On the way in it allows you to see all the memories, experiences and attachments that block the way and generate inner noise. Once you arrive, 'in silence', real peace is present, the trueness of your self as love is rediscovered.

Meditation as Communication

The context of all our lives is relationship. The currency of our relationships is our communication. At every moment we are sending messages to each other, whether we are aware of it or not. Despite the amazing technologies we now use to talk to each other across the world, our natural ways of communicating are breaking down. It seems we live in a globalized world as increasingly separated individuals in separated societies talking to each other from our separate and isolated terminals. Human communication is much more than just words and certainly much more than the 'packets of data' that we send down the line.

Real communication is filled with intimacy, real feelings and invisible messages. These messages are subtle and much deeper than words can ever convey. To commune with each other at these subtle levels is not something we learn in any academic forum.

This inner sensitivity and natural capacity for true intimacy is restored when we 'undevelop and undo' our habits of dependency on machines to do the work for us. This requires as much time in introspection and contemplation as it does in interaction. It is in meditation that we relearn how to cultivate, transmit and receive the kind of subtle communication that comes from the very heart of our self/soul.

Meditation as Creativity

The one capacity we all have in common is our creativity. It is, some say, why we are here! True creativity begins within your self. This is not self indulgent or escapist, it is the process by which you can choose the attributes of your own character. To meditate on patience is to create patience within your self, to meditate on a generous heart is to restore generosity to your heart. To meditate on compassion is to bring compassion to the reality of your life and the lives of others. In time, all those around you will benefit. This makes your personal meditation a gift to your relationships as you create and bring the best of your self to others.

Searching and Researching

Some people need a crisis before they will try meditation; other people need a friend to tell them how beneficial it is, while many will experiment simply out of curiosity. Each will likely seek a teacher to kick-start their meditation practice. Each will experience something ranging from a more peaceful mind to a more contented heart, from life changing insights to a deep personal enlightenment ...perhaps.

It is no surprise then that most practitioners seem to live a more peaceful, purposeful and joyful life. And it's also no surprise in the age of speed, stress and sensual overload that meditation is becoming more widely practised and therefore 'quite' rigorously researched.

And it seems it has been almost 'scientifically' proven to be rather good for you. Here is a random sampling of results of some research sent by friends and colleagues as they sought to get a more tangible hold on the benefits. It seems....

- Long-term meditators experience 80 percent less **heart disease** and 50 percent less cancer than non-meditators.

- 75 percent of insomniacs were able to **sleep** normally when they meditated.

- 34 percent of people with **chronic pain** significantly reduced medication when they began meditating.

- Meditators secrete more of the **youth**-related hormone DHEA as they age than non-meditators.

- It helps decrease stress, heighten memory and well, many other apparent benefits accessible at Dr Google and friends!

Ultimately these kinds of facts and stats are irrelevant in the face of personal experience, and that is always what any inner process of self-reflection and contemplation is about. You are the scientist, your consciousness, which is you, is your laboratory and meditation is the method of experimentation and exploration.

So, if the benefits are so numerous why are we all not rushing headlong to our nearest meditation center/teacher to learn how and integrate it into our life? One of the main reasons is probably addiction. As human beings we become addicted to three things - action, stimulation and emotion, sometimes they all come together. So we find it hard to see the value of sitting still in quiet, contemplative moments, within the busy schedule of an action packed, achieving lifestyle.

Or we find it hard to understand how being inwardly quiet and contemplative could be a happiness inducing practice when we seem to feel more alive and pleasurable when listening to our favourite music or watching a movie or just talking about a movie. Meditation puts our three drugs - action/stimulation/emotion - under threat.

That's until we are physically exhausted all the time or perhaps emotionally exhausted most of the time and our stimulations are no longer able to relieve or lift us out of our exhaustions. That's when we may seek the cause and deeper solutions. And that's when the undevelopment and undoing of the many perceptions and habits that keep us exhausted 'may' begin.

So it's probably true to say that most people will not experiment with meditation until they have to. It's not until their stress and unhappiness has reached such a level in their life that they are prepared to experiment with placing 'being' before 'doing'.

There is also a mythology that has grown around meditation that we sometimes use as an excuse to avoid sitting, doing nothing and learning how to be. Here are a few of those myths.

The MYTHS of Meditation.

1 You need to find a guru

No you don't. An experienced teacher to explain and guide is useful to begin with, but not a guru demanding blind obedience.

2 You need to be in isolation

Not true. It's best to learn meditation in the context of your current lifestyle and routines. Then, as you integrate your meditation practice into what you do now, you will enhance both your efficiency and effectiveness in daily life.

3 You need to close your eyes

Not necessary. It's best to keep them open (rest your gaze gently on a point in front of you) otherwise sleep may come and get you. Sleep is not meditation. Unfortunately!

4 You have to stop thinking

Definitely not. You may go beyond thought as you meditate, but it is not useful to attempt to force it. In the beginning the purpose of meditation is to become aware of your thoughts and then allow the quality and the quantity of your thoughts to change naturally. Being thoughtless comes a little later.

5 It takes years to learn

No it doesn't. You can learn in an hour with an experienced teacher to guide you. However, just like anything else, regular practice brings a greater and deeper mastery.

6 Meditation is the goal

Actually it's not. It is primarily a method to cultivate self-awareness so that the re-emergence of your true nature naturally undevelops and undoes all that is causing discomfort. There is no end point in the learning of meditation or the cultivation of your meditation practice. You are not 'going' anywhere!

7 You need to be in a group

Not strictly false. It helps a lot, especially in the beginning, to be in a group when meditating. The energy and atmosphere supports your practice and makes it easier. Ultimately the aim is to be in meditation anywhere, anytime. Why? Because meditation is a state of being, a state of consciousness, a state of awareness, not just something else on our 'to do' list.

8 Meditation is hard

Wrong belief. But if you believe it will be hard then so it will be ...for you! It's not easy and it's not hard!

9 You have to give up lots of things

Definitely not. Nothing is compulsory. However, if you do learn to meditate you will likely realize you want to give up old habits of unhealthy thinking, lazy lifestyle etc. But you make all the decisions.

10 It's very expensive

It's your choice. You can pay someone a lot of money to learn, or you can learn for free. Dr Google can help with either option.

A Visit to Inner Space

We all live in time and space. We've even conquered outer space – well some of it! But we forget to visit 'inner space'. To the practiced meditator inner space is always slow and tranquil to the point of *stillness*, always without boundaries and borders to the point of being aware of an unlimited *spaciousness* within.

Ask any experienced meditator and they are likely to remind us that it's only in this 'inner' space that we can find what we have been seeking in almost all the other 'outer' areas of our life – peace of mind, a contented heart and the wisdom to live harmoniously with others in this world. The journey there could be called meditation but there is in fact no journey because it is always only one second and no distance away.

Meditation - Getting Started

Expect nothing in particular to happen. But be interested in seeing whatever arises within the field of your awareness. It's not so useful to compare your 'insperience' with anyone else or to share your insperience with someone who is not genuinely interested. No two meditation 'insperiences' can ever be the same, so it's also best not to try to repeat them.

Meditation - The Absolute Basic Practice

- Sit somewhere you know you will not be disturbed
- Relax
- Concentrate your attention on your breath
- Follow your breath with your attention
- Become aware of what arises in consciousness
- Do not hook onto anything that arises
- Just keep observing
- Invoke your true nature, which is peaceful, loving and content
- Don't attempt to hold on to it
- Stop thinking about it
- Just feel it
- Keep watching what arises
- Allow any thoughts/memories that interfere to pass

- Notice whenever you are distracted
- Bring your attention back and start again

The Meditators Path to a Quieter World

There is good reason why many of us spend most of each day distracting ourselves with noise – whether singing or humming to ourselves, chattering to friends, family or colleagues, or leaving the radio or TV switched on. But it's only in the heart of silence that our most truthful inner voice can be heard.

When we are silent within, the mind is deprived of its major distractions i.e. the noise of the world out there. It becomes able to receive and reflect the natural attributes of our being. A heart that is silent and still, and a mind that is calm and at peace, is like a clearing in the midst of the noise and haste of a busy world, a place for expanding our subtle awareness of the deeper dimensions of the spiritual being that we are.

If you come across silent outer spaces, in the home or in the garden, or on walks in the countryside, be thankful for finding what has become an increasingly rare commodity. To use the gift of any quiet spaces properly, sit, be still within your self and experiment with the visualization that follows.

If occasional sounds interrupt the perfect quiet: think of them as ripples caused by beautiful fish nosing the surface of a still pond. Allow birdsong, gentle breezes and even more discordant sounds such as distant traffic, to pass through your mind like the wind whispering through a field of corn.

Similarly, with any thoughts that seem to arise from nowhere, if you simply observe them, without judgment or evaluation, they will fade into the background. They too will pass.

From Visualization to Meditation

An Oasis of Peace

Peace and quiet exist within all of us, but many of us have lost the knack of finding it. This visualization/meditation may help to release it from its inner source, and allow you to re-join it in your own inner oasis.

Try the exercise in either a quiet or noisy place – the effect will be the same.

- Sit comfortably, close your eyes and breathe deeply for a few moments.
- Visualize yourself sitting alone by the water in an oasis.
- The desert stretches beyond as far as the eye can see, but immediately in front of you is a fertile haven – your place of silence.
- Gaze into the mirrored surface of the water.
- Reflected you can see clouds passing in front of the sun.
- These are the thoughts, emotions and memories that prevent you from enjoying your place of silence.
- Banish the clouds mentally to reveal the unwavering light of the sun.
- Lean forward and look at your own reflection.
- The face you see belongs to a stranger.
- Is it happy or sad, alert or tired, confident or shy?
- Does it radiate energy?
- Now drink from the pool.
- The water is pure energy, the silent power at the silent heart of your being.
- Refreshed, you can re-enter your life

The Secrets of Self-Management

Your thoughts and decisions shape your destiny. This is not a new idea. A few moments of reflection reminds us that everything we create in our life, from the relationships we form to the work that we perform, begin as thoughts and decisions within our consciousness.

Wouldn't it therefore be ideal if we could simply have a few positive thoughts, make a couple of courageous decisions, and our destiny could be as perfect as we would like it to be? Real life of course doesn't quite work like that. There are many energies that we allow, consciously and unconsciously, to influence our thinking and decision making processes.

They include things like the environment, the weather, our current job, our family, our financial affairs, politics, culture and the most powerful, the media. All are waves of energy, which bombard us in different forms and at different times every day. Each has a different effect on our thinking depending to what extent we allow them in.

All have the potential to be what we use to confuse, complicate and pressure our self into unhealthy thoughts and not such good decisions. And if we are not careful we can easily use many of these external influences to shape our destiny. Obviously not a good idea.

And yet we cannot control any of them. They are all around us at every moment. All we can do is manage our self and therefore our thinking in 'relation' to them. This is why we need to cultivate self-understanding in order to practice the skills of self-management. The inner skills and abilities of 'self-management' are many. These are probably the most important to get started.

Detached Observation

Detachment gives you that 'space of time' to create a measured response and not be overruled by a habitual reaction.

It allows you to check your perception of what is coming to you and what is happening around you. And that can be as simple as seeing a situation as a problem or as an opportunity. Or it can be as deep as a shift from seeing the world as a dark and dangerous place to the world as an adventure playground.

That one inner shift alone allows you to stop taking things so seriously and start being more creative and playful. The art of detachment allows you to move from actor (watcher) to audience (participant) and back again, with ease – one moment just observing and getting a sense of things, and the next moment fully engaging.

This inner observational ability, sometimes known as 'detached involvement', means the world ceases to crowd your mind and randomly shape your thoughts and feelings. In learning to take time to just be watchful you can see with a deeper awareness, think with greater concentration and make your decisions with greater clarity.

By standing back internally and learning to watch life's flow you naturally become less influenced by all those forces over which you have no control. And in so doing there is weakening of the feeling that you are at the mercy of events, and an increasing sense that you have greater control over your own destiny.

More about attachment and detachment later.

Filtering Wisely

In the age of information overload, otherwise known as 'infobesity', it becomes essential to filter out what is of value and what is not. We find it hard to remember what was in the newspaper or on TV two days ago, simply because it had no value to us. Discerning what has value, which usually turns out to be very little, helps us not to waste time and energy. So much of the information that catches our attention 'out there' is simply stories about other people's lives, a form of local or global gossip, which we don't need to know. The rising tide of fake news also means so many of those stories are part, if not total, fiction.

By filtering out only that which is truly of value to us and not consuming or being consumed by the rest, we help our self to remain mentally fresh, emotionally stable and use our time and energy in the most worthwhile way.

Life is neither short nor long, but it is a span of experience in which we get an opportunity to create something that is both valuable for others and fulfilling for ourselves. If we spend that time consuming the creativity of others we will miss the opportunity to know and use the full potential of our own creativity. You may also avoid the fate of coming down with a bad dose of 'infoindigestion'!

Recovering Your Stability

You have probably realized by now that all your stress in life is self-created. You will be aware that your stressful thoughts and feelings are of your own making as you respond to people and events. You are likely to have therefore decided to take full responsibility for your 'ability to respond'. But still, certain people and situations are able to 'press your buttons' and you react emotionally, pushing your self off balance again.

At this point many induce within themselves a sense of hopelessness and give up the process of empowering themselves by restoring self-responsibility. They revert to old patterns in which they allow themselves to project onto others the suffering that stress is. They blame! But if you can practice recovering your stability you might eventually find your self stress-free in what were previously stress-triggering situations.

This means that when you do react stressfully and 'lose the plot' you then take time to sit quietly and center yourself. Where there is stress, where there is any form of 'reactivity', it means you are not in control, your emotions have taken over. There is some form of emotional disturbance, which can be likened to a storm within our consciousness.

But if you can learn to return to the center of your consciousness, to the 'eye of the storm', you will always find your peace and your power. Today that may take 10 minutes, tomorrow 8 minutes, the next day 5 minutes, and so on, until one day no minutes. It is this kind of sustained inner work that you get the chance to practice every day. Even the greatest saints and the so called enlightened masters would have practised this vital aspect of self-management in the face of the everyday changing textures and colors of the many varied scenes and personalities of life's rich pageant.

Humour

We would probably all agree with the sentiment, "Well sometimes you just have to laugh at your self". If we can't laugh at our self, and there seems to be many who can't, then we will tend to take life too seriously. All seriousness has fear behind it (you'll notice this in your meditative/reflective practice) and fear is what stress mostly is.

Can you learn to laugh at your self? Yes of course. But you may have to cultivate your, "What was I thinking", mindset. Your, "Silly me', sentiments'. Your, "Did I really say/do that", reflective chuckling.

A good place to start is in the bathroom. Lock the door, look in the mirror and just laugh at your face. You'll find the laughter a bit forced and a bit false at first. But if you stick with it, after about 30 seconds, you will start to relax and find your self giggling. If this doesn't work then you get your money back!

When you're finished watch out for those two men in white coats waiting for you outside.

Ride the Sound

Some of the oldest meditative practices are accompanied by chants or bells.

If you opt for this approach to your meditation, choose a sound that will fade gently to silence.

Then ride that sound with your awareness until you find your self in silence, allowing the calm that is always present within to cradle your inner self.

Eventually, with a little practise, you will be able to visit this inner citadel of quietness even amid the restlessness of everyday life.

II
A W A R E N E S S
P A U S E

Questions

Who do you think you are?

What do you think you are?

Where do you think you are?

Reflection

When you are managing your self:
a) what are you managing exactly

b) why do you think many people don't want to cultivate at this level
of awareness?

Action

Research Google for meditation courses in your area and then go
along and dip your big toe in meditation's waters, metaphorically
speaking!

Contemplation

"The goal of meditation is not to get rid of your thoughts and emotions,
the goal is to becomes more aware of your thoughts and emotions
so you move through them without getting stuck.
Then, once the mind is quieter the soul will speak."
Dr. P. Goldin

4

The Wisdom of
HAPPINESS

> "No one else is responsible for your happiness.
> Don't assign that much power to someone else.
> Happiness is an inside job"
> Mandy Hale

BEING Your Self is to BE Happy ...Naturally!

There is an idea, some call it an 'insight', while others call it obvious, that we, as beings of consciousness, start out like water begins its journey; pure and natural, free of all toxins or any form of pollution. In other words we each start our journey unconditioned, innocent, pure and emanating unconditional love.

After water arrives from the clouds above, over time, it starts to absorb and be polluted by a variety of toxins that it encounters in the air and on the ground. As a result, it loses its purity, its naturalness. Its original state is compromised. Similarly, our consciousness, over time, absorbs the toxins of fear and anger, sorrow and resentment, conflict and violence, from the world around us. We then learn to create the same mental and spiritual pollutants for our self.

We are now hyper-aware of all the toxins that our water contains. Many people spend large amounts money on water purification systems to ensure their physical health will not be compromised. They try to extract the seven toxins which, by many accounts, are now found in most tap waters; fluoride, chlorine, radioactive substances, pharmaceuticals, chromium, heavy metals and arsenic - but there are probably more!

Could it be a similar process with what we call happiness? Could happiness/joy/contentment be the original, pure and natural state of consciousness? Could it be that our consciousness has been polluted and compromised by a variety of toxins? That's the theory, but you cannot know the answer to these questions for your self until you check into the laboratory of your own consciousness and make your own investigations, test the theory, and see for your self. If you do then you 'may' notice the following.

The Toxins of Consciousness

Within consciousness the primary toxins are our beliefs. These are the beliefs that we seldom challenge, simply assume to be true and then create our own versions within our self. In this chapter we explore some of the most popular, polluting beliefs that are toxic to our wellbeing. You may recognize how they lead you to sabotage your happiness on a daily basis.

Have you ever noticed that everything you do, everywhere you go, everything you want, everyone you want to be with, are all motivated by one thing – the search for the holy grail of happiness? Almost everyone, consciously or subconsciously, is seeking happiness almost all the time. Hence the flood of books, seminars, courses, workshops and retreats in the last thirty years, all promising to restore your happiness. But none can. It's impossible. Here is possibly why.

The Three Mistakes

It's probably true to say that each and every day most of us will ask our self, consciously or subconsciously, "How can I, where can I, when will I, find happiness today". However, even with the creation of such questions few will acknowledge they are unhappy. Many of us become so accustomed to feeling some level of grumpiness or discontentment that we just learn to live with it believing that, well, this is it, this is my life, I am destined to feel like this.

It's the stimulations of life that then provide relief from this 'tolerable angst', while temporarily restoring hope that real happiness is just around the next corner. But there are a few who are ready to self-enquire with the question, "Why am I not happy now?" It's only when we ask this question, accompanied by a genuine curiosity, that our journey back to authentic happiness can begin.

Eventually there will be the realization of three mistakes that almost all of us are taught to make in life. These mistakes arise from beliefs that we assimilate from others and then recreate within our self.

First Mistake - Mixing Two Realities

The first mistake is to do with 'reality'! We all learn to confuse the *secondary* reality with the primary reality! The secondary reality is the world around us 'out there'. This is the ever-changing material world of people, events, circumstances and things, over which we have no control.

The *primary* reality is the world within us, within our consciousness, over which we 'can' have total control. This is the ever-changing internal universe of our perceptions, thoughts, feelings, emotions and attitudes.

We learn to 'believe' that the secondary reality, the world out there, is the primary reality and, for many, it seems to be the only reality. So we go looking for happiness in the material world around us, forgetting that happiness is an internally created state. It arises from within, but only when we have restored our true self-awareness. Only when we recognize the primary reality that is our own consciousness.

The Second Mistake - Confusing Pleasure for Happiness

When we cease to recognize that the primary reality is within our own consciousness, and therefore potentially under our control, we learn to believe that what we 'feel' is created by the world outside and around us i.e. by the secondary reality, which we have mistaken for the primary reality. Which, of course, is not under our control.

We then look 'out there' and go out there in search of the 'stimulations' that 'seem' to create the feelings of peace and happiness. We learn to 'believe' that our apparently 'happy feelings' come from outside in.

But those feelings are not authentic happiness, they are just moments of 'pleasure'. Moments that come and go. Moments that are unsustainable. So, the second mistake is we learn to 'believe' that pleasure is happiness. But it's only sensual stimulation.

So far so obvious.

The 'stimulations' that come from 'outside in' do give us a 'high' but the highs are always followed by 'lows'. Over time we need more new and longer stimulations to maintain the pleasure we mistakenly believe is happiness. Eventually 'the lows' become lower, longer and more intense. Otherwise known as suffering or 'unhappiness'.

That's why, when you believe the secondary reality 'out there' is the primary reality, and you believe that your happiness comes from the secondary reality 'out there', you will then go in search of pleasure believing it to be happiness and, as a consequence, you are guaranteed to make your self unhappy! You can easily check the veracity of that last sentence against your own insperience.

It's not that pleasure is wrong. It is part of the richness of life's many diverse experiences. It's just not authentic happiness. Or, if you prefer, it's not 'real' happiness. It's a fleeting, stimulated thrill!

The Third Mistake - Joining the Wrong Religion

Mistaking the secondary reality for the primary reality, leads to mistaking pleasure for happiness, which then leads to the third mistake. This is where the vast majority of us join the world's most popular religion without realizing it! Otherwise known as Hedonism! The hedonist is someone who seeks pleasure in life 'believing' it to be the 'only' happiness.

We inherit these beliefs mostly from parents and teachers who tend to show us how to make these three 'popular' mistakes every day. We mostly grow up in a culture that encourages these mistakes. And just about every business has a vested interest in ensuring we keep making these mistakes!

The Real Thing

However, we occasionally hear about people who become totally disillusioned with the 'pleasure seeking' way of life. They realize that it only leads to disappointment and unhappiness for some, misery and depression for others. Their suffering becomes so intense they start to question almost everything. Sometimes such individuals have an elevated position in an organization, much material wealth and a comfortable lifestyle. They appear to 'have it all', yet they feel empty on the inside, within the primary reality of their consciousness.

Then, one fateful day, they give it all up and 'convert' to the lesser-known 'movement' known as Eudonism! They realize that hedonistic happiness is just fleeting pleasure from outside in, whereas Eudonic happiness can be authentic and stable, as it arises from inside out!

They give up all their trappings and go and live and give on a Kibbutz, or they work for some obscure charity or for a volunteer organization, for almost nothing in return. In essence, they freely give their energy for the benefit of others.

When you meet them a year later one of the first things they often say is, "I wish I'd done that a long time ago". Why, because they rediscover that authentic happiness is a deep, self-generated feeling of contentment, bordering on a quiet joyfulness and sense of fulfillment, as a result of using their energy more 'meaningfully'. Usually by helping or serving others in some way.

Three Further Daily Errors

Until we become aware of these three basic mistakes, based on three common beliefs, we tend to make three further errors on a daily basis. Do you recognize any of these?

1 The Drive to Achieve.

You work hard, late and long because somewhere along the line you picked up the 'belief' that you have to work hard and achieve something in the world 'out there' in order to 'deserve' to feel happy 'in here', within your self. And if you don't work seriously hard then you should feel guilty and therefore extremely unhappy with your self!

Sometimes it's called the Protestant Work Ethic! Once upon a time this ethic was instilled in the minds of the many by the few, so that the few could benefit from the endeavors of the many. Religious doctrine was simply used as a way to transmit the illusion that happiness had to be earned and deserved. Naivety did the rest. It's not right or wrong, just the way things unfolded in less enlightened times.

But it's an ethic that now pervades many cultures and is glorified to this day. Hence the emphasis on achieving a certain status and/or material success in the world in order to believe you have 'achieved' happiness. Do you work hard in order to allow your self to feel happy?

2 The Beauty Myth

You are bombarded everyday by hundreds of images of perfectly formed, beautiful people. With immaculate figures, skin to die for and sparkling white teeth; you fall into the trap of the 'beauty myth'. It speaks to your conscious and subconscious saying, "If you are not absolutely physically gorgeous with perfect skin and the whitest smile you cannot be happy and successful".

So we learn to 'believe' that we need to spend time and money making our appearance pleasurable to others, in order to attract others attention and thereby gain their approval before we can be happy. Which is connected to the third daily mistake.

3 Making Others Happy

You become a people pleaser because you have come to 'believe' that you cannot be happy in your relationships until you do or say something that seems to make another happy! Without realizing we are each responsible for our own happiness, we are conditioned to believe others make us happy and therefore we make others happy.

It's therefore only a question of time when someone will become unhappy with your attempts to make them happy. At which point you will make your self unhappy because they are not happy with you. You will expect others to be and do exactly what you expect and only then can you be happy. But when they don't do what you expect you will make your self unhappy mistakenly believing that it was them that made you unhappy.

Phew!

In summary, here are the toxic beliefs that most of us will assimilate, carry through our lives and unknowingly use to make our self anything from a little to extremely ...unhappy:

1. The primary reality in life is the material world outside of our conscious self.
2. Pleasure is happiness.
3. Happiness is stimulated - it comes from outside in.
4. You cannot be happy unless you work hard and achieve.
5. You cannot be happy unless you look beautiful in the eyes of others.
6. Other people 'make' you happy and you 'make' other people happy.

7. Happiness can be found if searched for.

Which leaves us with two questions, what then is real happiness and how do we cultivate our happiness every day of our life?

There are probably three kinds of authentic human happiness. What we call contentment, joy and bliss. Each has its own necessary inner realization, perspective and perception before it can be created, felt and sustained from inside out. See if they ring true for you.

1 Authentic Happiness that is CONTENTMENT

Sometimes contentment is referred to as the deepest human happiness. If you ask the question why am I not content you will eventually realize that you, along with most of the rest of human race, have two particular habits that we use to kill our contentment many times each day. These are the habits known as 'judgment' and 'control'. The word judgment here refers to moments of disapproval and condemnation, which in turn underlie such unhappy habits as blaming, complaining, and criticizing.

Notice what happens within you whenever you detrimentally judge any of the following: a) what you yourself have said or done b) the words, attitudes or behaviours of another or c) what is happening in the big wide world. You lose your peace. Discontentment replaces your inner peace which is the foundation of contentment.

When you 'detrimentally judge' you are in resistance to what you or they have said or done. Where there is resistance there are the emotions fear or anger, although they may be somewhat subtle. And fear and anger, in all their forms, are what unhappiness is.

There are three levels of contentment that signify you have realized how to stop making your self discontented. This is what you 'can' do every day to maintain your happiness in the form of contentedness.

Contentment with Your Self

You accept your self as you are. You accept what you have said or done is gone, it's in the past and cannot be changed. You accept whatever you are feeling at any given moment and no longer think thoughts like, "I should not be feeling this or I wish I was feeling that". In other words, you stop judging and criticizing yourself and simply observe and 'be with' whatever thoughts and feelings arise.

This takes a little practice as you gradually become aware that you have thoughts and feelings but you are not your thoughts and feelings. You recognize no thought or feeling is good or bad but just 'what is' present at any given moment. This 'relationship' between you and your thoughts and feelings gradually enhances your clarity and decision making as to which thoughts to bring through into action.

Contentment with Others

You accept others as they are, as you find them, at every moment in every situation. You've realized you can't fix them or control them or make them do or be anything. They are not responsible for what you feel. You're free. You've realized everyone is doing exactly what they are meant to be doing at each and every moment. If it's your role to guide another e.g. you are a parent or manager, you are able to bring your wisdom to the relationship at the appropriate moments.

You know that if you don't maintain this perspective, then you'll spend a large part of your life trying to write other people's scripts and not write your own. Which means you're trying to live someone else's life for them and missing you're own. A classic contentment killer.

Contentment with the world

You accept the way the world is and the way you find it every day. This is not easy as so many of us have been raised to worry about the world, be anxious about what will happen in the world, and perhaps rage against the world. Try this more philosophical perspective partly inspired from Desiderata (google it).

Everything that is happening in the world is happening exactly as it should. Everyone is doing exactly what they are meant to be doing, everywhere, at each and every moment! All is unfolding as it should. All is well, even when it apparently isn't.

This does not mean we sit idly by and condone violence at any level. But neither do we rage against it. That just adds more violence. The rioters, or indeed anyone who is violent, are violent outwardly due to their own internal turmoil. They primarily violate themselves by sabotaging their own self-respect,. They are suffering and then express their suffering as violence towards others.

Each one of us is knowingly or unknowingly (mostly unknowingly) playing our own unique role in whatever 'scene' we find ourselves in at any given moment. If we can 'perceive' the grand scale of our collective drama on the stage of the world we may understand that each individual has a role to play. Even when that role contains violence towards others, it's still 'their role' at that moment.

Not an easy perception after a lifetime of cultivating the habits of fearing and judging, blaming and condemning. But it's a perception, an awareness, an understanding, that can restore a more peaceful and contented state of being thus allowing the emergence of a deeper wisdom and compassion to find their place in our consciousness.

Paradoxically it's such violent roles that we use to fill our movies and entertain ourselves. Then we condemn such roles in real life as if they should not exist. They do exist and will continue to exist. Perhaps all we can do is focus on our own role, our own capacity to create our own non-violent part of a larger world. Otherwise we can find a hundred issues every day that we can use to make our self discontented.

2 Authentic Happiness that is JOY

Living joyfully requires the realization of the purpose of life itself. 'Why am I here' is not an easy question to answer for oneself. The insight into 'why' often doesn't occur until you live in the question with tremendous interest and curiosity. One of the simplest answers, discovered and expressed by some, is as follows.

The purpose of life is nothing more or less than 'to live'.

But what does it mean 'to live'? If you contemplate this question you may arrive at an equally simple conclusion. The purpose of living is revealed by what you are doing all the time. It's the one thing you cannot not do, which is thinking, which is 'creating'. Everything you do begins with your thoughts. Your life unfolds according to the thoughts and decisions you create within your self. You don't come here to 'get a life'; you come here to 'create your life'.

We are all here to consciously create our life, our path, our journey, 'with' others, but without being mentally or spiritually dependent 'on' others. Deeply connected, but not dependent. And that begins within our own consciousness, within our self.

This is often not an easy insight as so many of us have been taught to expect to get a job, expect to get the money, expect to have a family, expect a certain lifestyle, expect to be looked after etc. Many of us learn to believe we are somehow automatically entitled to these things just by being present on planet Earth. We may even publically demonstrate and fight for our expectations and entitlements, sometimes known as 'rights'. But until we awaken to the reality that these are the things we are here to 'create' for ourselves we are likely to cultivate and live in a 'victim mindset' when any of our expectations are not met. It's a mindset, however subtle, that tends to become just another habit, thereby ensuring large chunks of our life will be joyless.

As we saw earlier it's our creativity that brings forth our joyful enthusiasm but if we have the habit of creating a 'victim consciousness' we sabotage and often extinguish that natural creative spark that lives in all our hearts.

To realize YOU are never a victim is no small inner task. Your body can be a victim of physical violence but YOU are never a victim. But are you aware enough to make that choice? That awareness arises when there is that clear sense of 'who I am'. But that requires the self-realization and self-understanding that we are not taught in school around the true identity and nature of 'self'.

Life is a creative dance between two energies, 'the physical' i.e. body, form, matter and 'the spiritual' i.e. soul, self, consciousness. Life is built on the accurate relationship between 'me' and my 'body'. That means 'you can touch my body, but you cannot touch me'. But if you believe you are just a body then you will believe that whatever happens to your body happens to you. That's when you lose the awareness that while your body can be hurt by something or someone 'out there', only you create your own 'hurt feelings', more accurately described as feelings of hurt 'in here'. Sometimes referred to as emotions.

Hurt in the body is pain, hurt feelings is suffering. Others can inflict pain in our body, but only we make our self suffer. It's just that it seems the vast majority of us are not aware that we have that choice. We are asleep to the reality that we don't have to suffer emotionally ...ever.

When we do suffer it's simply because we base our sense of 'who I am' solely on the form we call 'my body' and all the material things connected with our body.   And that's why we lose that joyfulness that comes with knowing your life is a creative process that is entirely in your own hands, metaphorically speaking. More about the connection between our sense of 'who I am' and emotions in Chapter 6.

When you realize 'you' are the master creator of your life you focus your attention and your energies on creating your own journey.   But without expectation of others or recrimination towards others.   Others are involved, relationship is the context, while we create and we also co-create.   We are 'in it' together.   So there is the participation of and with others.   But that can only be clean and accurate when we clearly know who and what 'I am'.

That's when you notice a 'quiet joy' arising from within your own being. This is the quiet joy that accompanies almost all creativity. Why? Because it's what we are designed to do. But it's best not to turn this idea into just another belief, but to see if this is true for you in your own 'insperience'.

3 Authentic Happiness that is BLISS

Bliss is that authentic feeling of happiness when you are a completely and utterly free being. Remember that feeling when you mastered your first bike and you were flying down the hill, with the wind in your hair, not a care in the world, and away from those 'big people'. Bliss! For a few moments at least.

The deepest freedom is obviously an inner state. When you are a truly 'free spirit' you are not anchored by anything, not attached to anyone and not trapped in any object, idea, belief or memory. If you ever live curiously in the question, 'why am I not happy now' it won't be too long before you realize it's because you sabotage your own freedom and entrap your self. Which is extremely unnatural.

DIY Prison Cell

As soon as we awaken in the morning the vast majority of us start rebuilding our inner prison cell in which we will spend the rest of the day. We will unknowingly learn how to lose our freedom of spirit and become attached to and trapped in one, if not all, of the seven primary phenomena that exist in the secondary reality that is the world 'out there'. They are position, power, pay, possessions, people/person, prestige and privileges. Each one is like another bar in our cell. We don't notice how we lose our self IN the ideas and images of each within the reality of our own consciousness.

Believing them to be sources of permanent happiness, and not realizing they can only provide temporary pleasure, we use them to build a false sense of 'who I am' without noticing they are actually the bars of our inner cell. Then we wonder why we spend much of our time in some form of fear. Fear of losing one or many. This is why so many of us create and feel some level of anxiety so frequently in our daily life. It's also why we often feel both overwhelmed and confined, as we sometimes think and even say, "I just feel as if I'm trapped".

The Bars of our Cell

1 Position

When you become attached to a position you identify your self with that position. You lose your sense of self in the 'idea' of the position. This can be in the formal context of an organization or the informal context of family or community. Positions can change, be threatened or be removed, which means lost. If you are attached to and identified with a position you will always create some anxiety in the form of feelings of insecurity. That's the fear that kills your contentment and certainly makes that quiet, abiding joy impossible. When you create the habit of identifying with a position then it's as if you don't have a position, the position has you. It's a habit that needs to be undone.

2 Power

Along with position comes power, apparently! This is a sense of authority over whom, in reality, you have no authority! This is what will shape your relationships with many others. You believe you are the one with the power and you then use that idea to form your sense of 'who I am' in relation to 'them'. That's one reason why some people feel powerful in some relationships but not powerful in others.

When you have the habit of defining your self by the power that you believe you have over others you don't have power, the 'idea of power' has you. It's a habit that needs to be undone if you want to be at peace within your self and with others.

3 Pay

Perhaps the largest of our inner prison bars is money. When you make your sense of security dependent on money you are guaranteed to make your self feel insecure. When you have monetary wealth beyond your needs it's hard not to define your self by the amount of money you believe you own, or by your salary level. Once again it's a habit to use this 'idea' to build our sense of self. Then you don't have money, the idea of the money has you! Undoing this habit is liberation from much anxiety.

4 Possessions

The illusion of possession runs the world. The desire to 'possess and own' runs the lives of the majority.   We learn to identify with material things as well as their style and brand. In such moments, which are often many moments in a life lived by the material paradigm, we are not being our self. We are lost in the images and ideas of what we believe we have that represent us.

Hence the old saying 'you don't have possessions, your possessions have you'. You become them in your mind but few are aware that they do so. It's a habit that needs to be undone if we are to be free ...again.

5 People

To be trapped in the idea or image of another is to lose your self in that idea/image. Sometimes we seem to love someone more when they are not present. Why? We 'idealize' them in our minds. We create a perfect idea/image of them and then lose our self in the idea/image. It really is 'all in the mind'. Then we call it love. But it's not love, it's attachment and misidentification. Once again, it's not easy to see this. It's often subtle.   But the confusion between attachment and love pervades our world.

Whenever we are attached to and identified with another person we are not so present for them. Our relationship is more with our idea of them and not the reality of them. The ideas and beliefs that we create about them become fixed and therefore our prison.

6 Prestige

Some years ago, for many, the first port of call after rising in the morning, was the bathroom, then the kitchen, then the lounge. Today, for many, the first pilgrimage place in the morning is more often the laptop and their Facebook page to see how many 'likes' have arrived overnight. Two likes and it's a depressing start, 42 likes and they are so happy.

We worry about what others think of us. In such moments we believe we are our reputation. We use what we believe others think about us to build our sense of identity. We are habitually trapped in an imagined prestige. In such moments we don't have a reputation our imagined reputation has us. This one habit alone is worthy of our focused attention to ensure it is undone.

7 Privileges

If we live anywhere in the so-called developed world we probably live a privileged life. At least compared to the rest of the world. But we take those privileges for granted. All the while making our self anxious and stressed if any of those privileges are threatened. And if they are not threatened we will imagine they are about to be, as we allow the media to feed us with the raw material to create our speculative worries that something is going to go terribly wrong very soon.

There are so many illusions built into this loss of personal freedom, from which arises an almost constant state of unhappiness, that it 'seems' we can only ever alleviate it with moments of pleasure! For many, it's probably true to say, a life of quiet desperation is survived by frequent sensory indulgences! How many industries thrive and become wealthy on the backs of our sensory indulgences?

But it's all OK. It just the way things have evolved up to now. The more aware we become the more we restore our true nature the more wisdom we can bring to our daily choices.

Illusions of Freedom

We believe we are free because we tend to believe freedom is defined only by the ability to go anywhere, say anything and do anything, buy anything ...that we want! But that's not true freedom. It's just a kind of physical freedom in the secondary reality 'out there'.

Freedom in the primary reality of our own consciousness is complete non-attachment from everything and everyone 'in here'. Paradoxically, only then are we fully available for anyone and everyone around us 'out there'.

When we are free on the inside i.e. non-attached, we are no longer busy with the emotions of fear and sadness (the most common forms of unhappiness) that must come with our attachment to any of the seven P's. Only then are we internally free enough to do the most natural thing with the energy of our consciousness, which is to 'create' our own ways of extending 'care' to others!

For many, such insights into why and how we make our self unhappy usually won't make sense until they become so tired or so stressed or so dis-functional in their relationships, that they are forced to stop and deeply reflect on the beliefs that are running their life. That's when we start to see those three mistakes! That's when we start to realize how the beliefs we are carrying are the cause of our search for happiness in the wrong places.

Mirror Mirror on the Bathroom Wall!

The toughest belief to expose and undo is that what you are seeing in the bathroom mirror is YOU! It's not! It is just a physical appearance and the authentic SELF is not a physical appearance.

Our physical body is where the secondary reality begins. If we invest our identity in anything in the secondary reality, unhappiness is our inevitable destiny. That's why, for many, their stress, their suffering, begins in front of the bathroom mirror every day!

So now you know why you are not so happy, perhaps! Now you know that to be happy it is necessary to be truly free, and that to be truly free you need to stop losing your self in what is not you. Only in that freedom, can you be your true authentic self! Only then are you non-attached and non-needy!

Only then can you be a true 'giver' and only then can you rediscover your authentic, 'eudonic' happiness, that comes from inside out, as you give of your self. Then, gradually, extremely gradually for some, the addiction to pleasure and the illusion that pleasure is happiness quietly fades away.

It's been so long since the vast majority of us have 'known' and lived this way, so long since pleasure and happiness were disentangled, so deep are the habits and tendencies to seek the short term pleasures, that it's going to require a little time and deliberately focused attention to restore one's self to that state of inner freedom.

That's why it's probably a good idea to invite your old friend 'patience' to join you on the journey back to simply being your contented self.

The 7 Habits of Frequently Unhappy People!

It's only when we realize and fully acknowledge that we are each 100% responsible for our happiness that we start to increasingly 'notice' the things that we do, many times every day, to create our unhappiness.

Only when we accept complete responsibility for our feelings will the habits that sabotage our contentment and joy start to atrophy. They are habits that many of us have learned to justify (a habit in itself!), as we often don't want to see and accept that we are each the cause of our own unhappiness.

Sometimes, we mistakenly call these habits 'natural'. They 'seem' to form the very fabric of our culture as they find expression in our day-to-day relationships. Here are seven of the most common unnatural habits that we use to make our self unhappy. See if you agree. If you do agree, take a leaf out of the Bob Newhart approach to 'self change' and just 'Stop It'. (see his hilarious sketch on YouTube)

1 The Habit of Judging

This one we have already 'exposed'. Not only do we learn to judge but close on the mental heals of our judgments often comes the 'sentence' and the 'punishment'! All together (judgment, sentence and punishment) make up the package called 'condemnation' which is a guaranteed killer of one's own contentment and joy! So 'stop it'!

2 The Habit of Criticizing

When you criticize it means you are in attack mode. Somewhere in your mental or verbal assault is the emotion of anger, albeit in a milder, subtler form. And when you are irritated, frustrated or angry you cannot be happy. Some of us attempt to justify our attack by calling it 'constructive criticism'. But if there is any anger present it's more often a disguised attempt at revenge or punishment. Definitely not a happy habit, but a common one all the same. Just 'stop it'!

3 The Habit of Complaining

It seems to be endemic in some cultures to complain. Complaining signals the presence of upsetness and therefore the absence of happiness. Whereas 'giving feedback' and 'making a request' ensures there is no discontentment. It's a response, as opposed to an emotional reaction. It's an easy theory, but hard to practice, especially if we have been playing that old 'complaining record' all our life. Are you a complainer? Stop it!

4 Blaming

Projecting blame onto someone else is not only a happiness killer it's usually a strategy to avoid responsibility. It's driven by the perfect combination of anger and fear and is therefore a painful cry that sounds like, "It's all your fault", which is code for, "I have just made my self very unhappy"! Go on, stop it!

5 The Habit of Arguing

Trying to prove you are right, or attempting to make the other as right as you, is usually both a tense and grumpy affair. Neither side is happy in the process. Even if it seems one side has won, any happiness is short lived until the next opportunity to 'be right' is craved for and invoked! To argue is to tell the world that you prefer misery to merriment! Stop it!

6 The Habit of Competing

It's not so easy to see why the habit of competing is an unhappy pastime. Most of us have assimilated the belief that competition is good, fun and even joyful. But all we have to do is glance at the faces of long distance runners, tennis players and even snooker players, and we will see more that 90% of the game is played in a state of toil filled tension with many moments of abject suffering. Occasionally, in the middle of the game or the match, someone will let a little joy slip out, but it doesn't last long. Almost all forms of competition contain fear by definition, fear of losing, which along with anger, are the sworn enemies of happiness. Are you a proud competitor in life? Try a different way. Stop it!

7 The Habit of Controlling

As we have already explored, attempting to make others dance to your tune is always an impossible task. Expecting the world to be and do as you would wish is an expectation too far. Both are demonstrations that you still believe others are responsible for your happiness.

That others should dance to 'my tune' is probably the most popular belief in the world. Only the enlightened soul has realized you can't control anyone, but you can influence. But to be influential it's necessary to divorce other people's behaviors from your feelings. Are you a control freak, ever? Guess what, just, stop it!

If this one truth were realized and lived globally i.e. that we are each responsible for our own happiness, the world would be a very different planet on which to live.

So there you have it. Only seven of many habits many of us will activate, sometimes several times each day. In so doing we repeatedly forget our personal happiness is a personal responsibility.

II

A W A R E N E S S
P A U S E

Questions

Which two of the 7 P's do you think you are trapped in the most?

List the 5 relationships in which you feel happiest then rate each one on a scale of 1 (pleasure dependent) up to 10 (non-dependent happiness)

Reflection

What do you think are the three key factors that seem to sabotage people's happiness the most? Contemplate and discuss with two other close friends.

Action

Pick a day when you will decide to be happy in every situation and every relationship no matter what happens. Then at the end of the day review the day and see if you can identify why you lost your happiness at certain moments in certain situations... without blaming anyone else.

Contemplation

"The foolish man seeks happiness in the distance,
the wise grows it under his feet."
James Oppenheim

5

The Wisdom of
SUCCESS

> "Don't aim at success - the more you aim at it and make it a
> target, the more you are going to miss it. For true success,
> like happiness, cannot be pursued; it must ensue."
>
> Viktor E. Frankl

Would you know success if you saw it?

Many, if not most of us have been conditioned to pursue success down
the fast lanes of career, achievement, fame or financial wealth. In so
doing we learn to narrow our focus on a limited definition of success,
and consequently spend most of our lives either in a race or in a chase!

The day arrives when the fuel starts to run out and both mind and
body begin to give us the 'slow down' signal, before it becomes too late.
Hence the increasing number of people, in an increasingly earlier age
group, are experiencing burnout. So it's no surprise that definitions and
perceptions of success frequently come under review.

The consequences of our 'success conditioning', based on achieving
and acquiring, that is the hallmark of the production and consumption
materialist model of living, can be far-reaching and deep. Not only can
it be a perfect recipe for a stressful personal life it easily 'spills' into
other areas of our lives. The disintegration of the family, the dilution of
our education, the destruction of our environment, the destabilization
of our climate, the polarization of the rich and the poor, are only a few
outward signs of the personal pursuit of success directed and defined
mostly by the material paradigm.

At a personal level the evidence that you may not be going in the wisest direction manifests as an almost perpetual anxiety, accompanied by a kind of unhappiness and emptiness that eats away at the soul. Even when people do reach the dizzy heights of achievement, hear rapturous applause or soak in huge wealth, there is almost always the feeling that something is missing. Even then, they may not make the connection between their unhappiness or emptiness and the idea that they may have taken a wrong turn in their 'pursuit of success'.

No one can tell you what success should look like for you. All you can do is absorb the various perceptions, review many sources of wisdom on the subject, then take some quiet time for your self to create your own definition/s and make up your own mind.

Here are a few insights to add to your contemplations.

Signs and Symptoms of Success – Part 1

Imagine your pursuit of success has been re-routed down a different path, perhaps a truer path. What 'might be' some of the signs that you are personally on the right road?

1 You have decided what you mean by success.

Before asking your self what success means, take a moment to reflect on the context in which you seek to succeed. In the context of **work** most people define success by status and salary, while others define it around meaningful relationships and job satisfaction. In the context of **family** some define success around just having a family, while others will define it as the creation and sustenance of a happy, harmonious, well balanced family unit, over a long period of time. In a **personal** context some people define success around self development and spiritual growth. While others define it around numbers of friends and material acquisition. And in the context of **life** itself, success is defined, by some, as survival, while others define it as being of service to society.

Suggestion; at least once in your life take a weekend, head for the hills and give your self an opportunity to sense and see and decide what success means to you. At the very least you plant the seeds of the right questions in your consciousness. They usually take time to bear the fruit of, "AHA!, now I see, now I know".

2 You have clarified your values.

As we explored earlier values are what you care about most in life. We all have a set of core/governing values. It seems few can readily identify them because we seldom take time out to consider what values really are, what our personal values are, and then articulate them. Even fewer, it seems, will align their aims/goals and intentions with their values and thereby create an integrated life. If you don't then what is 'sometimes' considered the deepest success i.e. being content with how you live your life, will be impossible. If you don't then it's likely you won't be the spender of the 'time' of your life, it's more likely someone else will spend it for you! Your time and energy will be harnessed to achieve their aims and their goals and bring their values to life. (see The Wisdom of Time Management)

3 You have chosen to affirm your choices.

Many of us have a tendency to make significant choices in our lives and then quickly forget we actually made the choice. The work we do is often such a choice. If we forget to re-affirm each day that we choose to do the work we do, it can easily feel like a daily chore. We may even start to think of it as a 'necessary evil'. Suddenly we are sustaining something we view with resentment in our life. Enthusiasm becomes a forgotten feeling as animosity and reluctance kick in. Not exactly the ideal ingredients in our success formula.

When you re-affirm past choices each day, you freshen your energy, accept responsibility for your life choices and bring a proactive attitude to your relationships. This energy then naturally attracts new options and choices down the line. If you can't re-affirm your past choices in the area of the work you do then perhaps it's time to ask your self why.

4 You have accepted responsibility for all your discomforts.

You have realized there are no justified resentments. You have realized that it's not what others say or do that makes you feel that way, it's what **you do** with what others say or do that makes you feel that way! They may try to insult and defame you, but you don't have to consume, digest and be affected by their poison.

When you realize you are totally responsible for all your thoughts and feelings then a) you begin to investigate and understand exactly why you create dark thoughts towards anyone or any situation b) you start to end all your darknessnesses (no small success in itself).

When you become absolutely determined never to have a dark thought about anyone or anything, more people, and indeed more opportunities, are naturally drawn to be in the presence of your radiantly peaceful, proactive, lightness of being. But you can only know that is true when you experiment for your self.

Let's push the 'pause button' for a moment. A story!

The Tourist and the Fisherman

While out walking a tourist sees the most idyllic scene: a man in simple clothes dozing in a fishing boat that has been pulled out of the waves and which has come rolling up the sandy beach.

The tourist's camera clicks, the fisherman awakens. The tourist sits next to the fisherman and launches into a conversation, "The weather is great, there is plenty of fish, why are you lying around instead of going out and catching more?" The fisherman replies, "Because I caught enough this morning". "But just imagine," the tourist says, "you could go out there three or four times a day, bringing home three or four times as much fish! You know what could happen?"

The fisherman shakes his head. "After about a year you could buy yourself a motor boat," continues the tourist. "After two years you could buy a second one, and after three you could have a cutter or two. And just think! One day you might be able to build a freezing plant or a smoke house, you might eventually even get your own helicopter for tracing shoals of fish and guiding your fleet of cutters, or you could acquire your own trucks to ship your fish to the capital, and then......" "And then?", asks the fisherman. "And then", the tourist continues triumphantly, "You could be calmly sitting at the beachside, dozing in the sun and looking at the beautiful ocean!" The fisherman looks at the tourist: "But that is exactly what I was doing before you came along!"

Inherent in this frequently shared tale of the tourist and the fisherman is the clash of two philosophies – the philosophy of 'more' which sustains the utopia of affluence, and the philosophy of 'enough', which creates the utopia of liberation.

The tourist philosopher is sure that doing more faster and at a larger scale will create greater affluence thus creating more time to do more of nothing! Seldom are the traps in this philosophy seen until after they have been sprung.

Trap One is that once more stuff has been created or acquired it requires more time and attention to maintain it and keep it safe.

Trap Two is the false concept of progress and the use of the modern servant of progress i.e. technology. The rise of the car is an example of falling through the trap door of 'false progress'. One philosopher puts our automotive history in what might be a truer perspective, "From the outset the car was hailed as the ultimate time saver, dramatically shortening the time it takes to reach a desired destination. But contrary to popular belief drivers do not spend less time than non-drivers in moving from one place to another. They travel to more destinations".

The power of speed is converted into more kilometers on the road. And time saved is reinvested into longer distances. From transport to communications time saved is transformed into more appointments, larger outputs and increased activity. Hours saved are eaten by new activities and the expansion generates new pressure for time saving devices and a cycle begins again. As a consequence, in one particular country, the average German citizen today travels over 15,000km a year as opposed to 2,000km in 1950".

Trap Three is an addiction to action. Mesmerized by the sophistication and apparent power of technology, we succumb to its promise to take us to the utopia of 'liberation from action', and the prize of 'more free time'. But the opposite happens as we become more like hurry addicts and rushaholics. In our dependence on 'speediness' most of us just end up rich in (technological) things and poor in time.

We don't notice the moment our busyness becomes laziness in disguise. Behind our busy and distracting activities with the so-called 'tools of progress', we are avoiding our self, the inner self, where time begins and ends for the self. This inner space is where timelessness can be found on the other side of a busy mind. Ask any experienced meditator and they are likely to remind us that real relaxation and renewal is only possible when hands AND mind are quiet and still for significant 'periods of ...time'. They will also remind us that if our minds are quiet and still, even when hands are occupied, we will have entered the gates to the utopia of liberation.

In the middle of the last century, somewhere in the Pacific Ocean, an island was discovered for the first time. The natives were found to be practicing the 'philosophy of enoughness'. As soon as they had done enough they stopped.

At first they were called lazy by those who discovered them, until someone pointed out that while they may be poor in things, they were rich in time. Striving and struggling for 'more' was a foreign concept to them. Simplicity and frugality lay at the heart of their easiness within themselves and within their culture. They were already living in the utopia of liberation in contrast to our time-compressed lifestyles in the utopia of affluence.

In the utopia of affluence the mind is not free, it tends to be busy with its acquisitions and speculations of future accumulations. Which returns us neatly to the second four of our eight 'possible' signs and symptoms of success.

Signs and Symptoms of Success – Part 2

5 You have a free mind.

In the utopia of liberation, success is a mind that is open to everything and closed to nothing. It is a free mind with all the time in the world. A busy mind is a closed mind and a closed mind means a mind that is attached to something, worried about losing something, closed around something or someone. Swinging through the jungle of our attachments within our own consciousness we don't realize how often we keep sacrificing our own mental freedom.

If your mind is closed you will likely be a person who is easily offended or disturbed. You may even be someone who is always on the lookout for reasons to be offended, for an opportunity to make your self upset by using what someone else has said or done.

The person with an open and truly free mind will not be easily offended, if ever. They won't 'lose the plot' emotionally as they don't lose their awareness of 'who I am', which is simply the awareness of a free spirit. A person who is truly free and open doesn't cling to anything or anyone.   And because they cling to nothing they are relaxed with everything.

Some would say such a level of being is impossible to achieve in this fast paced, materialistic and sometimes ruthless world. But if you can understand it, if you can comprehend and sense the freedom that lies in the above description, then you can 'be' in such an internally liberated state of being. Once again, it's best not to believe it, but to explore and experiment and see for your self.

6 You are a go giver.

You have realised that being a 'go getter' is the old paradign. It is an archaic conditioning of the utopia of affluence, and a diversion on the road to real success.   You are now a 'go giver' because you understand the law of cause and effect. You also know that at a physical level you cannot give what you do not have. But at a spiritual level the only way to know what you have within you is to give of your self. When you give the gift of your self in the form of your time, talents, care or simply your attention, with love, who feels that love first on its way out?   Which means if you do not give of your self unselfishly you will never know your self as love. You will never know love!

Whenever you say 'give me' you are actually imparting the message that you feel that you are not worthy to receive in a natural way. You are trying to force the universe to fulfill your desires. Desires that are usually born of the material conditioning around success. If you impart the message that 'I am not worthy' the universe will send it straight back in many shapes, forms and circumstances, which reflect your message.

In the utopia of affluence most of us are taught to live a life of gimmie gimmie gimmie - always striving, desiring, wanting, struggling to get something or somewhere, so that we may affirm our worth by a display of what we have acquired or achieved. In truth, it is a message to the world of our underlying perception of our worthlessness. It means we are still trying to measure our worth by material acquisition and have not yet awoken to our inherent pricelessness!

Ask the question - how can I serve? How can I make a contribution? The intention to serve will reveal what you need to give. If the intention is genuine it also generates the will. Then you will come to experience directly two inherent and unbreakable laws of life, the law of 'unlimited abundance' and the law of 'what goes around comes around'!

7 You know the song in your heart and that is your part.

You have discovered why you are here. Everyone has a song in their heart. It is their unique special note in the grand symphony of life. It is their purpose – their reason for being here. So many fail to listen to the song in their heart and therefore fail to find their purpose and therefore their part. Don't search for it, simply invite it, wait and listen for it to make itself known to you. Be open! It's not that someone else can tell you what your purpose 'should be'. It's what only you know it is!

What makes your heart dance and your soul sing?

Follow that trail.

Within the acorn there is a blueprint of an oak tree. Within your heart, the heart of your consciousness, there is a blueprint of what you are here to do. That's why your personal purpose is not created by ideas or images. It is detected and arrives in your awareness as one of your deepest intuitions.

8 You have set the past free.

True success will be impossible until you give up your personal history. So many seem to play the game of life only so they can have a 'distinguished past'. In so doing life ceases to become playful. They can't see that in trying to build a distinguished past they are displaying their own neediness for the recognition of others.

So they become absent from the 'here and now' and miss the richness of the moment as they swing between plotting future ways to enhance their reputation and looking back to replay the applause of yesterday. If you don't have a story you do not have to live up to it, and you are less likely to reside in yesterday. Embrace it and throw it away ...every day. As the old saying goes, 'the wake is the trail of the boat, not what drives it'. You are not your trail.

Success as a State

So what does it mean to be successful? At what level, in what context and by whose standards? If you were to give yourself some time to live in such questions you would likely arrive at the fairly obvious insight that, at the deepest level, success in life is not a material thing, it is not something that can be possessed, or won, or achieved or even attracted! It is a state of being. Some call it contentment, or happiness, or even peace. These are, for some, the deepest and most meaningful 'symptoms of success', but only when they are internally stable and consistent, and therefore not dependent on anything outside ourselves.

It sounds easy in theory but the tests and the challenges will come thick and fast. For example, can you act consistently with total honesty and integrity, thus generating a clear conscience without which the authentic happiness that we call contentment is impossible? You will be tested by those around you who would want you to compromise your integrity by acting against your values.

Can you remain peaceful and stable when all around you are in crisis or chaos? You will be tested by those around you who would want you to join them in their stressfulness.

Can you value others more than you value what you believe you possess? You will be tested whenever it's time for any object or person to leave your part of the field of play known as 'my life'.

Can you accept full responsibility for all your thoughts, feelings, words and actions? You will be tested by those around you who will encourage you react as if someone else made you think and feel.

Are you able to see past the weaknesses/mistakes of others and focus on their inherent goodness/strength? You will be tested by the influence of those around you who judge and condemn others for their weaknesses and transgressions.

Are you able to let go of the past? You will be tested by those around you who will want you to rake over the coals of the past and reignite old conflicts.

Can you give without the desire for anything in return? You will be tested by those who would measure and define 'you' by your material achievements and try to make you aware of the apparent greatness of their accumulations and achievements.

These are perhaps a few of the intangible measures of success. No one else can measure them except your self. One thing sabotages all of them. Your unacceptance of others, which shows up in your mind as the desire for the other to behave differently or just be a different kind of person.

As long as we desire to change other people and the world around us it means we are still trying to 'police the universe'. The enlightened soul however, has realized that is 'not my job'. They know that the light and power that emanates from a human being in a stable state, a contented state, from a giving intention, is the greatest and most influential gift to others and to the world.

But before you listen to anyone (including this book) it's probably worthwhile finding a tree, on a quiet and sunny hillside, by a peaceful meadow, next to a meandering river, to sit and gently reflect on what only your own heart can tell you in response to the question, "What does success really mean to me"?

It will of course generate many other questions. Like what is the purpose of my life? What do I value? What kind of success have I been pursuing up to now? Then, as many have said, that when it comes to this unique and special journey called life there is a time when asking the 'right questions' is much more important than having the right answers.

Success and Happiness

To add more fuel to your deliberations and feed a little more wisdom into your quiet contemplations, here are some insights and juxtapositions contrasting 'success and happiness' from a variety of different sources:

- Success may be earning lots of money; happiness is having people to spend it on.

- Success may be measurable; happiness is limitless.

- Success may be a fancy car; but happiness is a great ride.

- Success may result from working hard; happiness is bringing your joy to the work.

- Success may be the fame; happiness is the journey there.

- Success is maybe being first over the finish line; happiness is giving your best in the race.

- Success 'may' feel like being right; happiness is being true.

- Success is earned; happiness is inherent.

- Success is sometimes an award; happiness is its own reward.

- Success may be money in the bank; happiness can't be deposited.

- Success for most is seldom easy; happiness will never feel difficult.

- Success may require sacrifice; happiness is ever plentiful.

- Success may require late hours; happiness is all day.

- Success may be a second home; happiness is always home.

- Success may be receiving praise; happiness is never needing it.

- Success may be reaching the top; happiness has no ceiling.

- Success may be all the money in the world; happiness is needing none of it.

- Success is doing what you love; happiness is adding love to what you do.

- Success is usually always just ahead; happiness was never behind.

- Success is often envied; happiness is always shared.

- Success for many is a kind of perfection; happiness is embracing the imperfections.

"I think everybody should get rich and famous and do everything they ever dreamed of so they can see that it's not the answer" - Jim Carrey

II

A W A R E N E S S
P A U S E

Questions

What would you consider to have been your successes in
your life so far?

What does success really mean and look like to you in the various
'contexts' (home/work/leisure etc.) within your life?

Reflection

In your life, at the moment, would you say you are pursuing the
utopia of affluence or the utopia of liberation?

If someone was to watch you all day and every day what would
they see?

Action

Interview three close friends this week and ask them what
success means to them?

Contemplation

"Success occurs when opportunity meets preparation.
What are you preparing for"?

6

The Wisdom of
EMOTIONAL INTELLIGENCE

> "No matter the situation, never let your
> emotions overpower your intelligence"
> **Kushand Wisdom**

Emotional Intelligence or Emotional Confusion?

Could it be that 'emotional intelligence' is yet another oxymoron? When emotion enters, it seems intelligence exits! Our emotions sabotage our intelligence. This is hard for most to understand and even harder to see, mostly because so many of us have an unclear understanding of what exactly emotions are.

Most of us have come to believe that emotion can be a negative or a positive 'thing', but few venture beyond 'thing' and attempt to ascertain the exact nature and true cause of 'emotion'. We just take it for granted that emotions are either good or bad, and part of life's rich pageant. If challenged, most people reveal they don't really know what they mean when they use the words emotions and feelings. Those that think they do find it easy to disagree with others who also think they do.

Take a piece of paper and write down your definitions of emotion and feeling. Notice how it's both hard to define each and even harder to untangle them. Then try comparing your answers with those around you. Careful, you don't trigger an emotional argument.

Life is essentially a series of relationships, and the primary currency of exchange in all our relationships will be our emotions and feelings. This absence of clarity about the what, why and how of our emotions/feelings means creating, building and sustaining stable harmonious relationships can be difficult for many and a nightmare for some.

The Paralyzing Power of Emotion

Even our modern-day psychiatrists, psychologists, therapists and personal development gurus have differing and often confusing perspectives around this subject. In such specialist fields there is often a lack of clarity around the true cause of emotion, the toxicity of emotion, the addictiveness of emotion, the ability of emotion to drain your power, the paralyzing effect emotion has on your ability to think clearly, the havoc emotions can wreak as they sabotage your ability to discern accurately and make good decisions, and how eventually, emotion may kill your body.

All in all, there appears to be a fair amount of 'emotional confusion'. So the purpose of this reflection on EQ is to attempt to lift and clear away some of that fog. As we journey together into this extremely intangible territory of emotions and feelings the aim is not to convince you of anything. In fact, the opposite. Please do not believe a word you read. It's at the level of belief that clarity is easily lost. I invite you instead to test what you read against your own insperience.

See if you can see what I describe as something you are familiar with within yourself, not what you believe or have heard from others. You don't have to be a specialist in any area of psychology or therapy to understand the what, why and how of your feelings and emotions, only someone who is consistently cultivating and fine tuning their self-awareness.

In fact, if you rely on the academics and many of the so-called specialists, you may not learn a lot and find yourself being drawn up yet another theoretical, sometimes academic, garden path. The path may look impressive and even beautiful, but there is a good chance it will be a path to misunderstanding. The only path worth following is your own. So please put every word you read here up against your own awareness. If something is not clear my email is at the beginning and end of the book.

OK here we go. There is a good chance you are not going to like some of what you read and when you decide you don't like it you may 'feel' a little ...emotional! Remember that it's not me, or the words on the page, that's creating your emotion. It's you. It's always you. That's the first hurdle. It's called accepting absolute self-responsibility, which means every thought and emotion that occurs within your consciousness is created by you.

Consciousness is the Key

Many people associate emotions and feelings with the body and see them primarily as sensual events. While we easily notice the physical 'effects' of emotion in our body we don't tend to notice the 'cause' is within our consciousness, which is non-physical.

As we explored earlier we generally learn to believe that we are our physical form and that that's all we are. It's this belief that tends to ensure we don't see and understand the origins of our emotions. It's also why we find it hard to develop a clear insight into the difference between our emotions and feelings. We tend not to learn to become aware of 'where' we create and feel the emotion first, which is NOT at a physical level, but at a more subtle level within our consciousness.

In order to become aware of where and how emotions arise we need to deepen our sense of self. As beings of consciousness, occupying and animating a physical form, it's necessary to understand a little of how consciousness actually works. Just as the body has certain organs and appendages necessary to live in and navigate through the material world, so consciousness also has certain faculties that allow us to navigate wisely and live harmoniously in the world of our relationships. So, let's refresh and expand our understanding of the three primary faculties of the consciousness of every human being that we identified in chapter 3.

The Faculties of Consciousness

When you become aware of your self as consciousness you will see you have three faculties within your consciousness, within you, at your disposal. First there is your **mind**, which is like a screen on which you can create thoughts, images, ideas and concepts. Across the screen of your mind you run all the different 'relationship stories' of your life. Most are 'histories' that you rerun like old movies.

Then there is your **intellect**, which you use to 'discern' and evaluate the 'quality' of either your created thoughts/ideas or the accuracy of any 'possibility thinking', as you create your decisions. It's your intellect that you use to discern the false from the real, illusion from reality, accuracy from inaccuracy.

Then there are many impressions, which are memories of many actions that become your personal habits, traits and tendencies. These are recorded in what some have termed the **subconscious**. These habits and tendencies, created and recorded over time, form a subtle matrix that constitutes your unique personality.

The more you become self-aware, the more you meditate, the more what was in your subconscious becomes present to your conscious awareness. Just as your body has the faculties of hands, arms, legs and feet to get around the three dimensional physical world, so within your consciousness, within your self, you have these three faculties, mind, intellect, personality (which is rooted in the subconscious) that allow you to navigate the inner dimensions of thoughts, attitudes, decisions, choices, all the way out to your behaviour.

Unfortunately we have forgotten how to be the boss within our consciousness and have allowed these three faculties to boss us. We are only occasionally the master of our mind and intellect, and seldom the master of the tendencies/habits that arise from our subconscious. That's why we tend to react automatically when one of those subconscious tendencies is triggered and comes to the surface. Habitual reactions mean we are not able to respond consciously and choicefully. 'Emotion' is always the primary ingredient in any 'reaction'. During any 'reactive moments' you are not the master of your inner faculties, emotion is, as it floods your mind and hijacks your intellect.

Understanding How Emotion is Created

Having set the background to our investigation into emotions and feelings let's now get down to the task of sourcing, tracking and understanding emotion itself. In order to get to the original cause of emotion we need to bring our awareness to our self and see how we misuse our mind and create what is commonly called 'the ego'.

In some strands of Buddhism there is a belief that the 'self' is an illusory entity created by the ego. But it seems to be the other way around. The self is the creator of the illusory ego. The authentic self gradually loses its 'clarity of awareness' and, as a result, I/you/we create an illusory sense of 'who I am'.

How can you know this? Only by noticing that the self can exist (be aware) without creating an ego. Whereas the ego cannot exist without a self, without a conscious, sentient being ...being present! You can't be 'taught' this level of self-awareness but you can cultivate it for your self. It is the result of those practices briefly mentioned in chapter one, namely meditation and contemplation. All I do here is 'point', using words and concepts. If you look for your self, while using your meditation/contemplations practises, you will see for your self.

You have probably not yet learned how to meditate and therefore how to know who and what you really are prior to the identities given to you by others. This level of understanding wasn't on the school curriculum and our parents didn't know either, generally speaking.

So you may find this next part 'challenging' but do remember to put it up against your own insperience. I'm about to suggest and demonstrate that all emotion is created by the ego, which is another way of saying ego is 'cause' and ALL emotion the 'effect'. This is why emotion, any emotion, is 'unhealthy' and why there is no such thing as a positive emotion. Neither are there negative emotions. Love is not an emotion. But we'll come back to that.

Let's give a definition to the ego. Something we can work with so that we may see the inner mechanism by which it is formed, why it is the cause of emotion and the effect it has on our thoughts and behaviours.

I am aware that if you have thought about this, and indeed if you have studied any psychology, you may not agree with the following definition. This is what I would call a spiritual definition and the core of all things spiritual is founded in our sense of 'who/what I am'. Here's my definition. First the essenceful definition:

EGO is a false sense of self.

Then the longer definition that includes the mechanism.

EGO is created when 'the self' attaches to, and identifies with, any image, idea, belief or memory in the mind.

If you are aware in the moment that you become attached to anything you will also notice that you lose your sense of self, your sense of 'who I am', in the object of attachment. Not 'out there' but 'in here' in your mind. That's where attachment happens. Therefore, EGO is the attachment to, AND IDENTIFICATION WITH, any image, idea, belief or memory!

We do this hundreds of times every day.

Four examples:

1 "You stupid Fool!"

You react *angrily* to an insult when someone says, "You stupid fool", because you are attached to the idea, the concept, that you are intelligent and bright. Anger means you are suffering but it's you that creates the anger. When you know you are not stupid and not a fool, and you are not attached and identified with the idea that you are bright and intelligent, you would not create a false sense of self based on the idea that 'I am very bright and intelligent'. You would be egoless and therefore undisturbable. Any emotional reaction to any insult just means the ego is at work, usually on both sides!

2 "Get a Move on"!

You are *irritated* by the slow driver in front because you are attached to and identified with 'the idea' that they should drive faster so that you can drive faster, or you are attached to 'the idea' of being at your destination by a certain clock time. The emotion of irritation means you are suffering and you are the creator. If you understand and accept some people drive faster than others and that you cannot control your time of arrival at your destination you would be detached and not make your self suffer. You would not build a sense of self out of the 'idea' of being in a certain place at a certain time. You would, in those circumstances, be egoless, and therefor suffering (irritation) free.

3 "That was Terrifying".

You sit terrified watching the movie. Seems normal and what most people do as entertainment. But behind your *terror* you know the movie is not real. Yet you will invest just enough reality in order to indulge in the emotion of fear. You will bring the character into your mind become attached to and identified with 'them' (ego) and then generate the emotions they are generating and make your self suffer. If you stay in the awareness of 'it's just a movie', it's just a fictional story, you would not create fear but probably laugh, as you would be fully aware 'this is not real'. You would be egoless.

4 "I'm Right and You are Wrong".

You find your self in an argument with a friend. It becomes heated i.e. emotional. The emotion is a mix of *anger* and *fear*. Why? Because you are attached to and identified with your belief AND the belief that you are right. So you perceive their belief as a threat to you. That's why all arguments are just clashes of two egos as they generate and self-fuel with emotion and often end in physical violence.

In each of these examples there is an attachment to, and identification with, something (an idea, image, memory, belief) that is not the authentic self. This creates the ego, a false sense of self. It takes place entirely on the 'screen of your mind' as 'you' go into your mind and lose your 'self' in what's on your mind.

That then becomes another habit that we record and build in to our consciousness. It becomes a part of our personality. It follows that no matter what skills, abilities and capacities we try to develop, that development will always be sabotaged and limited by the habits of ego creation and consequent emotional disturbances. Which is why some sports people find that the development of their talent is sometimes restricted and suppressed until they realize they have to change something within their consciousness. That something is usually a recurring emotional disturbance that either drains their energy or sabotages their focus and actions. Often both.

Those of you who have been in seminars, retreats and modules with me will likely recall my favourite example. You have just taken delivery of your new Audi. As you drive down the road you pass a group of friends. In your mind you are saying, "Hey look at me, no don't look at me, look at the car, look at the car!" In that moment you want them to see the car but with you in it. The image you are projecting to them of yourself is Audi. Your identity, your sense of 'who I am' is invested in and shaped by the image of an Audi.

This is easily proved because all I have to do is walk up to your new car, run a coin down the paintwork, and how do you feel? A little upset? A small amount of anger? Perhaps outraged? Most people would of course be livid. You are in pleasure or pain? You are in pain, or more accurately, suffering. The suffering is called anger. Who creates your suffering, your anger? You do. It's not me that creates your anger. I just do my bit with the coin. Self-responsibility remember? So, let's do this very rationally. I scratch your car and you suffer. Which means you think you are a car!

In that moment you are under the illusion that you are a car. But you are not aware of it. Of course, the anger passes, as all emotion does.

Another example: let's say David is an artist, a painter. In fact, he believes he is rather a good painter and has been for many years. Then Mary walks in the room and says, "David, did you really paint that ugly thing at the exhibition in the local museum?" What does David feel? Devastated. He feels great sadness, which soon turns to anger, which turns to fear the next time he sees Mary, as he fears she may say something similar about his work.

Three emotions are generated, all because David is attached to and identified with the image of 'brilliant painter' in his own mind. But wait a minute. Is painter what he is, or what he does? It's not what he is. It's what he does. Are you what you do?

The simplest definition of Ego is therefore one word. It's a 'mistake'. We mistake our self for something we are not. It is a form of misidentification and, as we will see, this is where ALL emotion comes from. It is also the reason why ALL emotion is not healthy. Not bad or good, not negative or positive, just unhealthy, or a sign of unwellbeingness!

So why do we do this, why do we 'habitually' make this mistake, sometimes hundreds of times a day? We have simply been taught, trained, conditioned to do so. We learn from those who learned before us like our parents, teachers and friends. Many people are 'in the business' of ensuring we keep making this mistake. Those known as marketing and advertising executives make a living from sustaining this kind of illusion. That's why it seems so natural and why the idea of NOT getting angry when someone scratches your car, spills coffee on your new carpet or burgles your house, seems so ludicrous. But let's understand exactly 'how' it happens as we return to the three inner faculties of our consciousness.

The Subtle Event Called Attachment

Everything in life exists in two places at once. Out there in the world, and in here, in our minds. The Audi is out there on the street but when you look at it you bring it into your consciousness and put the image of the car up on the screen of your mind. That's OK because that is what minds are for. To receive, recreate and hold the images of objects in the world out there. You also need to think about the car and make decisions about the car, such as cleaning it, buying petrol and oil etc.

That's perfectly natural, but the 'mistake' is when you leave your inner throne, the center of your consciousness, and YOU go into your own mind, not only that, but YOU go into the image of the car that's on the screen of your mind. You lose your sense of 'self' in the image. That's why you may be sitting there in front of me looking like you are listening to me, but some of you are not, it's as if you're looking 'through me' because you're off somewhere in your mind, in your car that's in your mind, you're driving your new car down some imaginary street. You've lost your 'sense of self' in the image of the car. So, when I step outside and scratch your car it's as if I scratch you. You then scream in emotional pain, entirely of your own making, precisely because you have identified your self with the car. That's why you take it so personally.

In spiritual terms this is called attachment. This is why, from a spiritual point of view, attachment is the first step in creating the ego and why ego is at the root of all our suffering.

So, lets back up and see how we could fix it i.e. how to not make our self suffer. How could we not create emotional suffering when our shiny new car is scratched/damaged? By being detached or non-attached, in our relationship with the car. This does not mean we do not have a car, or run a car, even an Audi! It means we have changed our relationship with the car.

All our relationships primarily exist within our own consciousness. It means you realize the car is just that, a car. It is not you. It does not represent you. In fact, you do not possess the car. You get to use the car for a while and then someone else will use it. You have the car in trust. If you have realized this then you have a relationship of non-attachment with the object called car!

You are also aware that things happen to cars including scratches. It means you have realized and accept that cars are designed to be scratched, bumped, damaged, scraped and will eventually turn into a heap of rusted metal. That's a fact of reality in the material world out there. If you suffer because something happens to the car, or indeed any object, it means you are having another argument with reality.

So now you are detached from the car. You no longer use the image of the car to build your sense of 'who I am'. So, when something happens to your brand new shiny Audi you don't lose the plot. You don't create emotional pain for yourself. You don't create the emotions of sadness, anger or fear – the three main families of emotion. But then you may say, "Does that mean you let the scratcher get away with it"?

Answer, definitely not. That is if he is still in the vicinity. Then you are faced with two levels of choice. Level one is around the scratcher of the car and level two is around the car itself. Level one looks like this. You can approach mister scratcher and ask him if he will make good the damage. You could take his name and report him to the police. You could ask him why he did it and seek to understand him.

Level two revolves around repairing the car. Will you get the insurance company to pay, will you pay, will you take mister scratcher to court, will you just leave the scratch on the car, will you sell the car with the scratch on it?

Every situation in life has a set of choices going forward. Life is a creative process where we have the opportunity to 'create and assess' choice, hundreds of times a day. But why can you not create and assess all these possibilities? Because you are emotionally upset, you are angry, and anger completely shuts down both your creative ability and your capacity to discern. Possibility thinking, creative thinking, goes out the window when you become emotional in any way. Try it and see if this is true the next time you are emotionally upset.

When you see this you will see this is how we all sabotage our own lives, and we don't even know it. Why, because most of us have learned to believe emotions like sadness, anger and fear are perfectly natural. Which is like saying it's natural to suffer, to be unhappy. The physical equivalent would be to stick a knife in your leg every day!

But maybe the car is not the problem for you. Maybe it's the money, it's the time, it's the inconvenience of having to get it fixed, it's the disrespectfulness of the scratcher. Then your attachment is to the image of the money, or it's to the image of doing something else with your time or it's to the idea of always being respected by others. The emotional suffering is still your creation because you are attached to an image which you have placed on the screen of your own mind and in which you also lose your sense of 'self'.

On the one hand, what is emotion and why do we become emotional is a huge topic. But on the other hand, it's simple. All our emotional disturbances are caused by some form of attachment/ego. It's complicated until it's simple.

The three main families of emotion are sadness, anger and fear. Whenever you create these emotions you are making your self suffer. It's not right or wrong, it's not bad or good, it's not that you should or shouldn't. Try not to judge and condemn your self. (or me or others!). That's just the ego again. They are all the result of a 'mistake'. A case of mistaken identity. The result of attaching your self to an image/idea/belief/memory in your mind. The mistakes become habits. All mistakes can be corrected, all habits can be undone. But first it's necessary to become 'aware' of the mistake. That comes with time and those practices mentioned earlier, such as meditation, contemplation and reflection.

The Difference between Emotion and Feeling?

How often do you hear this question, "Well HOW do you 'feel' about that?" In media interviews, in movie scripts, in our cappuccino conversations, 'how do/did you feel' is often the first and most repeated question. But it's a question that usually means 'WHAT' did you feel? HOW do you feel is a separate issue. We all learn HOW to spell, HOW to wash dishes, HOW to drive a car, etc., but it seems very few of us learn HOW to FEEL! In fact it could be argued that no one learns HOW to feel i.e. how to consciously choose your feelings, because no one teaches us! Could that be because no one really knows?

And then there is another question, which sits between the WHAT and the HOW of feeling. It's WHY do you feel what you feel! Once again it seems few people, when asked these questions, can clearly see *the what, why and how* of the one ability we all share as human beings, the ability 'to feel'. Complicating things even further are the emotions that we feel! When we 'feel emotional' what are emotions exactly, and why are we ...feeling them? There appears to be two reasons most of us don't clearly know 'what' we are feeling, most of the time! The first can be found in our education and the second in our body!

An Absence in our Education

The missing ingredients in our formal education were self-awareness and self-understanding.   There was no focus on understanding what we were feeling and why we felt what we felt. There was no separation between our emotions and feelings. This meant we didn't talk much about the inner world of our 'self', of our consciousness. We didn't discuss our feelings ...much! Perhaps we talked occasionally about extreme emotions like excitement or sorrow, but we said little about the more subtle and frequent emotions we were feeling in between. That meant we didn't develop a language to describe what was going on within our consciousness, where all our deepest feelings originate, accumulate or repeat.

Emotions in Body

The second reason we don't know 'what' we are feeling most of the time is we don't generally register our feelings until they have some 'effect' in our body. We don't notice how they originate within our consciousness and not in the form we occupy.

We often don't notice the emotional disturbance called worry until it has an effect in our stomach.   We don't notice the emotional disturbance called fear until our heart starts racing. We don't notice our anger until our fists clench and our face is hot! By the time we notice these emotions they often just feel 'physical'. So we fail to notice that the origin of the emotions that we feel is in our own minds. And if we do, we'd often rather not! Preferring to project responsibility for our emotional suffering onto others.

Without a Language

When we don't fully develop a language based on our description of the emotions that we create and feel, we don't develop 'shared meaning'. That's why most conversations around understanding emotions don't go very far, don't last very long and often regress either into an argument or the glazed look of boredom!

We don't start with, "Well what do you mean exactly when you say 'emotion'?" And very often, when we do ask the question, 'what do you feel about that', we really mean what do you 'think' about that! We don't realize we really mean 'thought'. Then we become confused and emotional, and end up wondering why we are feeling so ...agitated!

So, for many of us, emotions, feelings and thoughts become brilliantly entangled.

Read ten different writers on the subject of emotions/feelings, and you will likely find ten different perspectives and perceptions. It all adds up to a fogginess about WHAT we are feeling, which stops us seeing WHY we are feeling what we feel. And we need to see WHY if we are going to know and understand HOW to feel and be the master creator of our feelings...again!

An Unresolvable Catch 22

It's fairly obvious to most of us that we now live in a highly 'emotional' world. It seems many people live in an emotional state most of the time so that 'all' they are feeling are their emotions ...most of the time! And when they are not they want to! This diminishes our clarity around 'the what' and 'the how' of our feelings. Why, because in order to clearly see and understand the WHY and the HOW of feeling we need to be free of emotion!

When you are angry you cannot see that the cause of the anger is ...in you! In the middle of your sadness or fear you can't see the cause of your sadness and fear is ...in you! So you won't be able to see exactly WHY you made yourself angry or sad or fearful, as long as you are in those emotional states! Therein lies a good example of a Catch 22.

It also explains why the practice of meditation becomes so useful, as the purpose of meditation is to untangle ones 'self' from all emotional disturbances in order to restore the mastery of your feelings!

When you are 'Feeling Emotional'

So what are emotions exactly and what is causing us to 'emote' so much? See if this rings true in your 'insperience'.

All emotion arises from the ego (false sense of self), which is the result of attachment to and identification with that which is not me. Notice, when you are attached to anything or anyone, and something happens to what you are attached to, you create a disturbance in your mind, the primary faculty of your consciousness. That 'disturbance' is called emotion. The Energy of you is in an exaggerated **Motion**. So here is a definition:

Emotion is a disturbance in the energy of consciousness when the object of attachment is damaged, threatened, moved or lost.

In the previous example of the scratched car, someone damages the car and we create a disturbance in our consciousness called anger. We create and feel the emotion of anger. Why, because we are attached to and identified with 'my car'. But we don't react emotionally when someone else's car is scratched as we are not attached to their car and don't 'identify' with their car.

The perfectionist creates and feels the emotion of 'irritation' when the table is not laid out perfectly because they are attached to an image of how it 'should be'. The football fan becomes excited or sorrowful depending on whether their team or the other team scores a goal. Why, because they are attached to and identified with the image of their team.

A close friend dies and we become very sad, extremely sorrowful, maybe even angry, if we perceive someone else is to blame. Why, because we are attached to the image/idea of that person in our own minds. Unfortunately we learn to call that an expression of our love. But love doesn't make us cry, generate sorrow or anger!

So this is the mechanism by which we create all our sorrows, angers and fears. It's not bad, it's not that you shouldn't, it's just that we don't understand the mechanism, the process, by which this happens within our consciousness, so we cannot consciously choose to respond in another way. But now you do understand, perhaps, in theory at least.

The Cycle of Suffering

There is an 'emotional cycle' in which we all become trapped. It goes something like this. Fear arises, which then turns into sadness, which then turns into anger and back into fear. Why? We create fear in its many forms, such as anxiety, tension, worry, panic, terror, because we imagine (believe) we are about to lose something or someone (in the **future**). All fear is fear of future loss.

We create sadness in its many forms, such as sorrow, disappointment, downheartedness, melancholy, because we believe we have just lost something or someone (in the **past**). All sadness is due to the perception of past loss.

And we create anger, in one of its many forms such as irritation, frustration, resentment and hate, the moment we look outwards to find someone or something to blame for our apparent loss. They all have one thing in common which is 'loss'.

The 'belief' that loss has happened or loss is about to happen to something we are 'attached' to is why we create and 'feel' all these ...emotions! And therefore, why we suffer so much. The loss of the shininess of our car, the loss of the way the table should be laid, the loss of my football team, the loss of another person, the loss of respect from another.

Where there is the 'belief in loss' there must be a belief in possession. That shows up in our thoughts and words when we think or say 'that's MINE'. That's MY car, MY house, MY money, MY partner, MY family, MY country, MY belief! These are the most common attachments. That means that attachment (the belief in possession) is the pre-condition to a perception of personal loss and therefore the root cause of our emotions of fear, sadness and anger.

If we were not attached to anything or anyone we would not 'fear loss', we would not experience loss and we would not create and FEEL the emotions of sadness, anger or fear. We would not suffer. We would not make our self unhappy! If you're interested you can test this many times a day by taking a few moments to reflect on the emotions that you felt when you 'believed' you were are about to lose or had lost something!

Familiar Families

So, while the most common 'emotions' fit into one of the three 'families of emotion' - sadness, anger and fear, guilt and shame, also the result of the ego, are a combination of all three. We'll come to love and happiness, joy and serenity, which are not emotions, but 'natural' states of consciousness, in a moment.

It appears that many, if not most of us, will live our entire life in and out of this cycle of suffering, but we won't be aware of it. And we won't do anything about it because we learn to believe these emotions are both natural and caused by someone or something other than our self. We conclude there is nothing we can do and nothing we need to do about them. Until of course they reach an intolerable level. At which point the therapeutic professions may gain some of our hard earned cash.

But when we fully realize that we create all our own emotions we also see they are like signals, telling us we are acting against our true nature! One of the dictionary definitions of emotion is 'agitation of mind'. When expanded to include the mechanism by which we create any emotion it sounds like this:

Emotion is a disturbance (agitation) in our consciousness (mind) when the object of attachment is damaged, threatened, moved or lost! (which are all forms of loss).

Once again take a few moments to test this in the light of your own 'insperience'!

At this point many ask, "But what about love and happiness, are they not emotions too"? This is where we fully enter the territory of 'emotional confusion'. We were never taught how to be aware of our emotions and feelings. We were not shown how to clearly identify the emotions that we create and feel. We didn't learn how to differentiate between 'feelings' such as love and joy, compassion and serenity. And we didn't do the inner work of disentangling such feelings from our 'emotions'. So these deep and natural feelings (feelings of our true nature) were lazily labeled and seen as just 'other emotions'.

This leads us to believe all our emotions are just naturally occurring states of consciousness. We didn't realize that any agitation (emotion) in our consciousness is a signal that we are out of alignment with our true nature, we are making a mistake (attachment/possession) and that there is something we need to change (let go of) within our self if we want to liberate our self from suffering.

Are love, peace, joy and serenity agitations? Are they forms of suffering? Or are they natural? They are of our true nature. In other words emotions are unnatural. Not bad or good, not right or wrong, just unnatural. The result of not being our authentic self!

Emotional confusion is where we confuse a state of agitation within our consciousness with a natural state of consciousness. Common 'emotional confusions' include: worry is confused with care, we worry about someone because we believe to worry is to show care! But worry is fear and care is love, and fear (agitation) and love (natural state) cannot co-exist, they are at the opposite ends of the feeling spectrum.

Love and fear are made of the same energy, which is the energy of our consciousness, our self, they are just different vibrations of that energy. Fear is love distorted by attachment! Once again you can test this in the light of your own insperiences.

We confuse excitement with happiness. But excitement is a 'stimulated agitation' within our consciousness, whereas true happiness is contentment and a natural emanation of joy from our heart (the heart of our consciousness) into the world. Happiness is not agitation. We confuse respect with fear, passion with anger and terror with relaxation as we consume the latest horror movie.

This is why we use the words 'love' and 'happiness' a lot but really mean something else. It's just that we are not aware that we mean something else because we don't 'accurately' know what these words mean! When we use the word love we usually mean attachment e.g. I love my car, I love my house etc., really means I am 'attached' to the house and car. I love coffee, I love chocolate, usually means I am 'dependent' on a substance to stimulate certain physical feelings. In the movie there is usually a moment when he looks into her eyes and says, "Darling, I love you". But what does he really mean? Often it's with that look of longing, meaning 'I want you'! In such moments love is confused with desire.

There is a similar absence of meaning around happiness as it is confused with acquisition, with pleasure and with relief from pain e.g. the toothache has gone I am so happy! That's not happiness it's relief.

So it's no wonder we are thoroughly confused about what we are actually feeling most of the time. This results in an inability to read the signals that our feelings/emotions are sending us. So how do we unconfuse our self? Understanding the process of feeling goes a long way. So let's explore what 'feeling' is, exactly?

There is a very simple definition of feeling.

Feeling is perception by touch.

Each of us can perceive, touch, and feel at three levels – the physical, mental/intellectual and spiritual.

Physical Feelings

When you touch the new dress or suit at the department store you *feel* the material and you *perceive* the quality of the material. So you 'feel' it, at a physical level, using your physical sense of *touch*! It's a physical feeling.

Mental Feelings

You also 'feel' at a mental/intellectual level. As you read or hear some of these ideas you bring them into your consciousness, put them up in your mind and create your own versions of what they mean. As you do you *perceive* them, you *feel* them. It's as if you 'touch' them with your attention. A little voice inside says, "Yes that feels logical, I perceive the logic in that", which is YOU using your **rational** ability to perceive/feel.

At other times you don't see/perceive the logic, but still that little voice says, "YES that feels right, that rings a bell. I don't know why but I get it!" In this instance you are using your **intuitive** capacity to perceive/feel something. These are what could be called subtle feelings at the mental/intellectual level. Notice you CANNOT do either (perceive/feel rationally or intuitively) when you are emotional i.e. when there is a disturbance called 'emotion' in your consciousness!

Spiritual Feelings

Our deepest capacity to 'feel' occurs at the spiritual level when you 'pick up' the invisible radiant energy of another. We feel their vibrations, often without seeing them or even being in the same room. We sense their mood.

But the deepest level of 'spiritual feeling', the subtlest of feelings, is to sit quietly, withdraw all your attention from the world around you, away from your own body, quieten your mind, and you will become naturally aware of your own inner peace.

In such moments you are in your natural state of peace and you 'feel' that peace. You touch, perceive, feel, your own natural inner peace. Hence the practice of meditation is to release the self from gross physical feelings and even the more subtle feelings at a mental/intellectual level, and to be in a deep state of silence and stillness. In this state you naturally feel your true underlying nature, which is cool, calm and contented. But you don't 'think it'. It's just a feeling that you are immersed in. In such moments you are it.

And when you come back out of that deep feeling, back into thought and action, you notice that you are refreshed and recharged. Not physically but spiritually. The signs are many, including increased clarity, a greater sense of freedom and a renewed intention be more giving in your relationships with all others.

Restoring Choice

So why don't we choose our feelings in this way? Because we were mostly taught to believe that feeling is a 'noun' and that it's something that 'happens to you'. But it's not, it's a 'verb'. It's something that you do! But no one teaches us 'how to feel'!

"When you are emotional you cannot choose your feelings"

When you believe that feeling is just a noun i.e. some 'thing' that comes to you, you start searching for certain feelings that are stimulated by some 'thing' or someone 'out there'. That's what eventually takes you into a state of dependency and perhaps addiction. Which is why most of us are addicted/dependent on something or someone.

Let's bring feeling and emotion together and, as we do, we notice two things.

1 Feeling Your Emotions

You do feel your emotions, and it seems we are almost constantly seeking, creating and feeling some kind of emotion, simply because emotions are addictive! It's an addiction that the marketing, advertising and entertainment industries exploit to make their money! Our emotions are mostly triggered by external events. Not caused, but triggered. It's not the event but what we do with the event within our consciousness that causes our emotional agitations and reactions.

2 Restoring Choice

You can free your self from feeling emotional i.e. you can stop creating emotion, and if you do you will notice that only then are you able to consciously 'choose' what you feel. But as long as you are addicted to certain emotions you cannot be the master of your ability to feel and therefore your feelings. So when you are emotional (creating and feeling emotion) you cannot 'choose' your feelings. For example when you bring anger into a meeting you won't be able to generate a feeling of forgiveness when someone admits a big mistake. You won't be able to choose to feel compassion for someone in the meeting who is suffering. You won't be able to be calm and focused for someone who needs your calm and clarity to help them with their confusions. Why, because you remain internally busy, agitated, creating and feeling your emotion of anger.

So, in summary, emotions seem to be what most of us are creating and feeling most of the time. It's a habit. They are addictive as well as exhausting. We don't learn to see and know the difference between emotions and feelings. All emotions are forms of suffering although they may not feel like it at the time. They are unnatural disturbances that begin within our consciousness. But because we also call our natural states of being, such as love and happiness, emotions, we then believe anger and fear are also natural, so we are unlikely do anything to understand and change them. And as we are conditioned to mistakenly believe that other people and events cause our emotional suffering we don't take responsibility for the emotions we create and feel.

The cause of all emotion is attachment to something within our consciousness. That's why all emotion originates within our consciousness around the perception of 'I have lost' or imagining 'I am going to lose something' or 'they made me lose'. We are attached to so many things, people, places, beliefs etc. This is why we live in an almost perpetually emotional state of fluctuating anxieties, sorrows and angers.

In reality, when you are being your authentic self, feeling is something 'you do', NOT something that happens to you. To be the master of your feelings, to be able to consciously choose what you will feel, requires detachment or non-attachment. Detachment does not mean you do not care or that you avoid. It does not mean you 'go cold'. In fact you cannot care for another fully unless you are detached.

Which Side of that Fine Line?

It's often a fine line between being emotional and being emotion free. Only you can ever know for your self which side of that line you're on. Even when you seem to be speaking and acting without any emotion, but with warm feelings towards someone, you may have brilliantly learned to disguise your emotions.

So let's break it down and see if we can help our self become more aware of our emotional reaction (emotions always tend to be reactive) versus our loving responses. Let's see if we can find the line and notice when we step over it as we oscillate between our emotions, which always have root cause in some form of attachment, and our loving responses, which arise from our true nature which is ever present but temporarily lost to our awareness.

According to the understanding outlined in this chapter so far, the following are what I call emotions. They are the most common emotions we all tend to create on a daily basis.

Anxiety, tension, worry, panic, terror, fearful - all forms of FEAR. Sorrow, depression, hopelessness, melancholy - all forms of SADNESS. Irritation, frustration, anger, rage, resentment, hate, jealousy, envy - all forms of ANGER.

Guilt and shame are both a mix of all three - anger, fear and sadness. Not so easy to see but if you retrospectively contemplate moments when you felt guilt or ashamed you will be able to spot the presence of all three, to varying degrees.

Excitement is, believe it or not, an aspect of fear. It's the other side of the fear coin. Both are agitations of your consciousness triggered (not caused) by some external stimulus. Notice when you watch anything competitive and you take a side (attachment) you are excited but also fearful at the same time. They come together. They are together. Forever! Subtle, isn't it?

You will always find the root cause of such emotions in some form of attachment (therefore ego) within your own consciousness. Once again 'they' don't teach us this in school mostly because 'they' were not taught so they did not know. So this really is 'see for your self' territory. I've already given a few examples of the relationship between ego, attachment and emotion in this chapter, but if you need more do let me know.

The Great Untangling

So what exactly are your natural states of consciousness? In other words states where there is no attachment and therefore no disturbance within your consciousness when you are 'in' and express these states.

Compassion, empathy, respect, trust, forgiveness, care - are all aspects of LOVE in action, love in expression. You will not be able to be in these in a loving state and give your energy in these ways if you are emotional. Notice when you do give your energy in these ways who 'feels' the energy first on its way out towards the other? You do. So these are what you might call 'powerful feelings'. That's because they're natural, consciously intentional, clear and focused. But as soon as you become emotional these feelings dissipate and disappear. Some examples in a moment.

Serene, calm, quiet, relaxed, tranquil - are all aspects of your natural underlying state of PEACE. Bliss, joy, contentment - are all aspects of your natural HAPPINESS, your natural 'joy of life', your joie de vivre. It exists in all our hearts (consciousness) but is frequently sabotaged by our emotions. Gurgling babies tend to have this natural joy (when they're not hungry or need their nappy changed) but as they grow, as we grew, they lose it, we lost it. Why? Yes, you guessed, we learned 'attachment'!

Real Life Examples of the Line Being Crossed

1 Listening Calmly

Your daughter is telling you of her achievements at school that day. You are listening calmly and caringly (peacefully and lovingly). But then, in the background, the news on TV is telling you that the price of petrol is going up. Suddenly you start creating and feeling frustrated, even angry. And when you do all your feelings of calm and care just disappear. Why? Because you are 'attached to the idea' of your money! Suddenly you cannot give and feel loving care because you have created the emotion of anger.   But the anger passes, as it always does, eventually, and you are able to return to your natural state of peacefulness and lovefulness, as you listen calmly and caringly to your daughter's day.

2 Creating Offendedness (yes I know there is no such word!)

You're in a meeting with your team at work.   You're listening patiently to many points of view.   Sometimes calmly facilitating disagreements between members of the team.   You feel cool and calm and warm towards everyone in the team.   But then one of the team refers to old people being a waste of time and energy, and in the way of acquiring more business. Suddenly you feel resentment arising. Why? Because your parents are old and in need of round the clock care. You are attached to a) your parents and b) to the 'idea' that old people should not be ignored or sidelined just because they are old.

However, your resentment destroys your calm, caring and patiently attentive acknowledgment of everyone's point of the view in the team. You've lost your effectiveness as a facilitator until you are able to put the 'image/idea' of parents or your 'belief' that old people not be callously regarded etc. to one side. (detachment).   Only then can you access and feel your true and powerful nature and return to calmly, warmly and sensitively facilitating the conversation.

3 How Dare They!

You are driving along while having a light and happy conversation with your partner next to you.   The sun is shinning, you feel naturally contented and the conversation is naturally flowing as you naturally share openly and lovingly with each other.   Then another car cuts you up at the lights and suddenly you are very angry. You are no longer able to feel loving and caring towards your partner, until of course the anger subsides, the emotion subsides, and you are able 'to be' your natural open, caring and loving self again. What were you attached to? The idea/image of everyone driving as respectfully as you.

4 I'm so Worried

You're talking to you friend about how much you care about your son. You're feeling naturally loving and warm about your son and towards your son. Even though they are not in the room. Then you notice the clock and they are 45 minutes late home. Suddenly your care turns into worry, your love turns into fear. You create and feel the emotion of fear in the form of anxiety and start creating all kinds of mental scenarios where something may have happened to them. Then they walk in the door and the fear disappears into relief, which seems like happiness, but it's not true happiness. Just relief from your self created suffering. Notice, when you do worry about someone, who are you really worried about? Worry is fear and fear always means an imagined future personal loss. What do YOU fear losing when you worry about someone else while believing and thinking that is how to care! Answers, especially from mums and dads, on a postcard to...

Our Fluctuations

Sometimes in certain situations and scenarios we fluctuate back and forth, in and out of an emotional state. One minute we are agitated and disturbed and the next minute we are calm and caring. Then a few moments later we cross the line again for another emotional upheaval. It seems most of us can tolerate this 'tooing and froing' for most of our life. Some say, "Well this is life, this is the way it's meant to be". Others however just get tired, as emoting is tiring. Or they get fed up with always being in sorrow, or anger or fear. They reach their own point of 'enoughness'. They see it's just become their habit to be unhappy and miserable. Each of us has a different threshold.

The best news is that you don't have to fight and struggle with your emotional tendencies. You can cancel them out by reawakening and restoring your awareness of your true underlying nature as a human being. *Love, peace and happiness* was the mantra of the hippies. They were right. But they had the wrong method.

The way back to 'being in' and feeling your natural states requires a combination of what has been termed spiritual practices i.e. meditation, contemplation, application and contribution. Gradually you will become keenly aware when you are becoming attached and how you are creating a false sense of who you are and why that is the root cause or any personal stress and suffering in your life.

Gradually it becomes easier to allow your natural states to shape everything from your intentions to your thoughts, from your attitudes to your behaviours. Eventually the habit of attachment disappears and the ego is no more. Liberation occurs as you come home to your self.

Emotional disturbances that express as **REACTIONS** Origin: Attachment/Ego	Non-emotional states of being that allow you to **RESPOND** Origin: **Your True Nature**
FEAR. Anxiety, tension, worry, panic, terror, fearful	**LOVE** Care, compassion. empathy, forgiveness, respect, trust, acceptance, openness
SADNESS Sorrow, depression, hopelessness, melancholy	**PEACE** Calm, tranquil, relaxed, quiet, easiness
ANGER Irritation, frustration, anger, rage, resentment, hate, jealousy, envy	**JOY** Happiness, contentment, bliss
Guilt - Shame - Hopelessness Excitement	

They are not opposites, although by positioning them this way it may seem so. Your true nature is simply distorted by the mistake of attaching to and identifying with what is not you! The result is emotion.
Both of the above lists are by no means complete.
What would you add and where?

II

A W A R E N E S S
P A U S E

Questions

1 What is the connection between the ego and emotion?

2 With whom do you find yourself slipping into 'reactive' mode most easily and most frequently? List three people and identify the attachment in each case.

3 If someone asked you tomorrow about the difference between emotions and feelings what would you say?

Reflection

Imagine you have accepted that your true nature is peaceful, loving and contented, what difference would that make to your intentions and behaviours towards your family and colleagues?

Action

Ask three people at home or at work what they perceive 'emotional Intelligence' to be. Write down and gather their answers.
Then deeply consider the question and write your own.

Contemplation

"Emotions are our main motivation,
that's why the world is in a terrible state."
Ian Lavender

7

The Wisdom of
DETACHMENT

"It's a paradox to the western conditioned mind that you cannot
know love and be authentically loving
unless you are non-attached."

Carolyn Max

Having explored attachment in the context of how the ego is
created and sustained let's take a deeper look at the what, how, why and
where of attachment itself. Attachment is a powerful strand running
through most cultures and communities in the world. It's hard to
conceive of a life without attachment. It's an emotive topic that easily
triggers much resistance.

How Detached Could YOU Be?

It's probably true to say that 'detachment' gets a bad press! In
Western so called developed societies it tends to be interpreted as either
'non-caring' or as some form of 'avoidance' and often invokes a feeling
of 'coldness'. Sometimes we may even use these interpretations to give
our self permission to avoid investigating the true meaning and
implications of being detached i.e. living from a place of 'non-
attachment'. And yet it's common knowledge that people employed in
many areas of 'service to society' such as the police, doctors, nurses,
counselors and therapists, are all taught to be detached as part of their
training. In other words, it's an essential inner practise in order to
discern the suffering of others, express genuine compassion and extend
the appropriate care.

So, what is the difference between attachment and detachment in reality? Attachment originates entirely within our consciousness. When we become attached to any 'object' or any 'person' or any 'place' or any 'idea', it takes place in our minds. We lose our 'sense of self' in the image/idea of the object of attachment within our minds. It's as if we leave our throne at the heart of consciousness and go 'into' what is on our minds. This can be for five seconds, five minutes or fifty years!

It's not that we are holding on to these 'things' with our hands. You can be holding tight physically to something or someone and not be attached. That's why to fully understand attachment it's necessary to understand what you do IN your own consciousness ON your mind.

Just as you are not your body, neither are you your mind. As we explored in the last chapter, it's on to the screen of your mind that you bring up the images of objects, people, places, ideas and memories that you then attached your self to. This 'mental location' of attachment is one of the reasons why detachment is so misunderstood. Few of us learn to be aware of exactly what we are creating and sustaining within our own minds.

This is why, when something happens to the object of our attachment in the world 'out there', such as cars and houses or clothes and other people, we take it personally and create suffering for our self 'in here' within our consciousness, within our self. While it 'looks' like something is happening to the object of our attachment 'out there' it 'feels' like it is happening to us 'in here'. We take it personally.

If we did not lose our self in the image of the object/person in our own mind we would be 'detached' and therefore able to remain undisturbed whenever something happened to that object/person. Not uncaring, just undisturbed - that's the tricky aspect that we need to disentangle. You cannot 'be caring', which means loving, unless you yourself are undisturbed by ...emotion. (Otherwise you'll need someone to care for you!)

It's only when you are undisturbed that you can extend caring accurately, all the way from intention to action. If you are (emotionally) disturbed then you are busy with your own disturbance, busy with your own emotions, which then get in the way of being able to extend compassion and care to others

This 'mistake' of attaching our self to an image or idea or memory or belief then becomes the basis for the creation of 'fear' in the form of anxiety and worry, as we project possible loss or damage to what we are attached to, into our imagined futures. ALL fear arises because we are attached to something, or in the case of the scary movie when we identify with the person in the movie who is attached to something/someone and is about to lose that something/someone. That 'something' often means 'their life'!

Unfortunately we have also re-interpreted 'worry' as care (fear as love) and have learned to 'believe' that if we don't worry it means we don't care! Not wanting to be accused of not caring we make sure others know that we worry. Then we worry that they may not recognize how much we care! So we worry some more and 'justify' our worrying in the name of care!

Sabotaging Our Freedom

So, attachment means we have 'trapped' our self 'in' the image of the object of our attachment in our own mind. Hence the incessant 'thinking about' the object/individual of attachment and whatever is immediately related to it/them. This then becomes a major source of mental tiredness, which can quickly translate into physical fatigue, as we think (worry) too much. This goes some way to explain why so many now live, and tolerate living, in almost perpetual anxiety. And why many seem to be 'tired all the time'.

It's well known that our physical health can be affected by the unwellness of our being. Attachment generates fear in all its forms and fear is 'unwellness of being'. Through the psychosomatic connection fear then has a huge effect on the health of our body. When you are not well in your being it's safe to say the underlying cause is attachment to something or someone in your mind.

Intangible Attachments

We also become attached to the images of less tangible 'things' like our beliefs, especially to the beliefs that were assimilated at a young and more innocent age. Hence our tensions and irritations that arise when we are challenged by others beliefs directly or indirectly. Each day we witness various levels of violence in various parts of the world simply because groups of people are collectively attached to a set of beliefs.

They believe it's right to 'believe' and they believe their beliefs are right and others wrong.

They believe their beliefs are the truth, but can't quite see they are simply attached to an idea/s or a concept/s and are therefore setting themselves up to suffer. Most of us can only recognize our 'belief attachments' when we start to argue about anything, but only if we take a few moments to reflect after the emotional heat of the argument has cooled.

Even then, we don't really want to admit we made our self suffer by being attached to a set of beliefs. For many there seems to be no alternative to having, defending and fighting for their beliefs. This is now an extremely prevalent mindset and obviously does not bode well for the future of many societies on our planet!

Violating Our Self

Attachment in itself is a form of violence upon the self. During the past few years we have become more aware that there are those among us who self-harm and self-abuse at a physical level. What is seldom recognized is it's not strictly self-harm, it's 'body harm'. But that doesn't make sense until there is the realization 'I am not my body'. Real self-harm occurs within our consciousness. Most of us have learned and practice self-harm daily at a spiritual and mental level i.e. within our consciousness, when we 'attach' our self to an image/idea/belief and attempt to 'live in' that image/idea/belief.

The signs of that level of 'self-harm' are the emotional states that we ourselves create when something happens to our attachment/s. But most of us don't want to recognize that we are responsible for our own suffering and therefore that we are self-harming. So we glorify both blame and revenge which allows us to continue our self-harming ways.

Anger and fear are addictive, so suffering becomes addictive and therefore self-harming becomes addictive. One way to sustain the addiction is to add pain to the suffering by harming the body. Another way is to mistakenly decide our angers and fears, sorrows and sadnesses, are natural. What could be better than naturally occurring addictive emotions that we can continue to self-create! It's like saying hard drugs are deemed natural and healthy and you can grow them in your garden and share them with your friends.

Learned Detachment

It's therefore no accident that surgeons are often not allowed or won't operate on their own family, as 'family' tends to be our deepest attachment. It is where attachment is most often mistaken for love! The emotions (tension and anxiety) that arise would therefore interfere with the surgeon's decision making ability and their capacity to remain calm, stable and accurate as they deliver the medical care that their profession has trained them to do.

It's also no coincidence that counselors and therapists are taught to be detached so they may give the highest possible care to those whom they serve. It is this juxtaposition of 'detachment' being necessary in order to 'care' that confuses most of us simply because it often seems the world in general, and certain industries in particular, make it their 'business' to keep us in a state of attachment in the name of care!

Personal Takeaways

When you become attached to anything or anyone it also means you are 'on the take'. You want something or you believe you are getting something vital to your happiness from the object of your attachment, usually through some form of 'stimulation'. But it's a stimulation that gradually, if not instantly, becomes a dependency, and therefore not the route to authentic happiness.

Detachment requires the ending of wanting and taking. Only then are you able to truly give and share (love) without expectation. This dynamic shows up in the art of 'detached involvement'. It sounds like an oxymoron but in the context of your relationships detachment allows you to be involved more fully and to engage more authentically, care more lovingly.

When you are attached to someone or to a particular outcome it's the 'wanting' something for your self that gets in the way of being able to engage, listen, feel and deeply sense what the 'other' is going through. Only when you are internally free from that 'wanting', which usually includes some 'neediness', can you sense, which often means 'intuit', the real needs of the other and perhaps meet those needs at that moment.

Perhaps this is why the art of 'detached involvement' has become a recognized management/leadership capability. It is an ability that allows you to let go of any personal desires, at least while you engage. It allows you to be free of all preoccupations on the inside, enabling you to be fully present with people and situations that require your attention. Whether you are playing your role as manager, parent or just good friend, 'detached involvement' enables you to nurture and sustain your relationships free of selfish concerns and with a genuinely benevolent attitude.

Practicing the Art of Detached Involvement

The value of restoring authentic detachment or non-attachment and the practice of 'detached involvement' is best understood within the metaphor of going to the cinema.

There you sit, in the auditorium, aware of your self patiently waiting for the start of the movie. When it does begin and all those colored lights start dancing across what was a blank white screen you may notice how you 'seem' to leave your body in the seat and go into the story on the screen. You get lost in the story and eventually lose your self in the characters. What they are feeling (usually an emotional disturbance) you recreate in your consciousness and you go through that same emotion. You live vicariously through them. Some more than others of course!

What few of us notice in such situations is that the movie isn't really playing 'out there' on the cinema screen. That's just flickering lights on a flat screen. The movie is really playing on the screen of your mind. You use the images on the screen 'out there' to create your own version of the story 'in here'.

Then you 'go into' the story and into the characters on the screen of your mind as you create your versions of them. This is 'where' the attachment takes place. Attachment is not a static thing! Attachment is a dynamic, changing, moving process within your consciousness as you continuously 'lose your self' in what is 'on' your mind.

And what are most frequently 'on' your mind are usually stories about others, situations and objects that you then create 'in here'. Yes, people, situations and objects etc. are 'out there' but your versions of them are your 'imaged creations'... in here!

As you bring what is happening around you in the office, at home, in the newspapers etc. into your consciousness, you re-create all that is 'out there' on your mind 'in here'. Then you lose your self in your creation of the world, the office, the home etc. 'in here'.

As a consequence you become extremely vulnerable to the inevitable change/s that take place in the world, office, home etc. And when changes 'out there' do happen it's as if they are happening to you. So you take it personally and become 'agitated' in your consciousness. This agitation takes various forms of emotion as we saw in the last chapter. It's those emotions (sadnesses/angers/fears) that keep you busy within your self on the inside and less available, sometimes partially available and often not available at all, for others.

Watching Your Own Movies

When you're busy losing your self in your creation, and suffering the consequent agitations, it's a sign that you are attached to, and trapped in, the stories that you create and project onto the screen of your mind. Being fully available and present for others therefore requires that you 'detach' and cease creating and losing your self in your stories. This is only possible when you are able to remind your self that the stories you run in your mind are 'only stories'. They are not real. They are memories. They seem real but they aren't the reality of this moment now.

This partly explains the rise in the popularity of mindfulness these past few years. We are beginning to recognize that we lose our self in our stories and become carried away in the thoughts and images that constitute our stories. We are neither fully present for others AND we are exhausting the energy of our consciousness.

Mindfulness is essentially a practice that reverses and undoes that habit. That's why the simplest definition of mindfulness is 'present moment awareness'. It's those moments when yes, you may have a story running in your mind, but YOU are able to detach and just watch it, observe it, and not get lost and caught up in it. This allows you to be fully present for those around you. This is detachment as an inner action, an inner state. No one knows what you are doing. You're not saying or even thinking, "Aha!, now I am detached". But both you and they will notice and feel you are being 'fully present' for them.

Let the Stories go

So, if you want to be fully present in the reality of now, which is the only reality, then it's necessary to stop creating and losing your self in your stories, in any story. For most of us, that's not so easy, simply because we have been creating and losing our self in our 'stories' since childhood. The habit is deep, so it's a challenge to undo.

Just as the director of a Hollywood movie does not mistake the movie they are making for reality, yet the making of the movie is real, so to, if we want to stay awake and aware, fully present here and now, it's necessary to realize our stories, our memories are not real. They are only 'representations' of a past reality filtered and distorted through our experiences and beliefs and therefore they are not authentic. They are not the reality of now.

Just as the movie you watch in the cinema is an illusion of an illusion so the stories you run in your mind are illusions. If you want to prove that to your self try describing the same memory one month apart. You will find it's slightly different each time. Reality cannot be memorized and recreated, only 'versions' of reality, which, by definition, are not real.

Internally Free

So the practice of detachment from your inner movies eventually slows the movies/stories down and the habit of creating them atrophies. In this way you learn to keep your self internally free and therefore your intellect (your 'third' eye) is free, 'non-reactive' and unclouded by emotion, allowing you to 'discern' and create the most appropriate 'response' to whoever or whatever you are facing. This is why 'detachment' is the bridge from knee jerk reaction to a measured, conscious and creative response.

Can you sit in the cinema watching the movie without losing your awareness that it's just a movie and therefore not reality? The happening called 'watching the movie' is reality, but the story and your version of the story, is not real, in the truest sense of the word reality.

Can you remain in the awareness that you are just an observer of the unfolding story and not get lost in the plot? Just as you are aware that it's just flickering lights on a flat cinema screen, so too, in the auditorium of your consciousness, you are aware that there are many thoughts in the form of images passing across the screen of your mind. But you are fully aware that there is YOU and there is the screen of your mind that contains the thoughts and images.

Are You Emotionally Addicted?

However, if you want to continue to be 'emotionally agitated' it means you're probably addicted to the stimulations that will trigger your emotions. Most of us do tend to be addicted to some form of emotional agitation, which is why the idea of detachment can easily be perceived as threatening the supply of our emotional drugs! It's our addiction to these emotional 'drugs' that keep us creating 'dramas' out of nothing and keeps us habitually attached to some story on the screen of our mind.

It's the search for our emotional drugs that disconnects us from others OR has us trying to push the other's buttons to get them to react emotionally so that we then have an excuse to do the same! In such 'scenarios' we become what we sometimes refer to as 'drama queens'! This is why 'detached involvement' is ultimately the foundation of true friendship, great parenting, effective leadership and our ability to help, counsel, coach and motivate others in both formal and informal settings. Only in a state of detachment or, if you prefer, non-attachment, can clarity occur.

See the Signs

There are seven signs of 'detached involvement' in action and therefore in someone who has freed themselves from both the emotional suffering and the emotional addiction that arises from all forms of attachment.

1 Warm and Receptive

In the mode of detached involvement you don't get sucked into the dramas of others or live vicariously through others. You are able to listen to their stories without being emotionally affected. It's as if you are warm, open and receptive while being calm, cool and collected at the same time. Not an easy state of being to maintain when the 'other' often expects you to mimic and join in their emotional turmoil and perhaps affirm their victimhood.

2 Responding Creatively

In the mode of detached involvement when it's time for things to 'leave' you, things like your job, money, people etc. you do not suffer emotionally. It's not a 'bad' thing if you do suffer, as emotional pain is not a question of good or bad – it's just a 'signal', and therefore an opportunity, to investigate the cause of your suffering. As all emotional suffering is ultimately self-created it means that if you can find the root cause (always attachment) then you can set your self free. If you want to! You can then make the shift from emotionally reacting to creatively responding and your inner choice is restored.

3 Present Moment Awareness

In the mode of detached involvement you are able to be fully present for others in the moment we call 'now'. You no longer create a fictional story and waste energy in worrying about what may happen (what may be lost) and therefore what emotion 'you' may 'feel' in the future. Worry is always speculative fear based thinking about losing something you are attached to... in the future. This can range from specific things or people, from an argument to levels of comfort within your lifestyle etc. The end of worrying signifies you are near the end of being 'absent' and the restoration of being fully 'present'.

4 Prejudice Free

In the mode of detached involvement your intellect is free of the bias and prejudices that were the result of your attachment to deep and often subconscious beliefs. You cease to filter the world 'out there' through the beliefs and perceptions that you were once attached to 'in here'. You can discern cleanly and clearly exactly what is going on!

5 Easy Does It!

In the mode of detached involvement you may set out to achieve a goal but if you don't arrive/achieve on time you don't beat your self up. You don't start your 'I am a failure/non-achiever' self-talk. You are not 'attached' to the outcome, so your motivation and enthusiasm is fear free and therefore much more sustainable. When your happiness ceases to be dependent on reaching your goals the journey truly does become the destination and now you can 'appreciate' all the views and experiences along the way!

6 Internally Free of Agitation

In the mode of detached involvement while you may have expectations of others your happiness is no longer dependent on anyone meeting your expectations. You are no longer dependent on others behaviours to 'make' you happy. You are free of any internal agitation and that freedom allows your natural happiness to arise from inside out.

7 Calmly Available

In the mode of detached involvement no person or event in the world can shock or shake you. You know that 'stuff happens' and as a 'detached observer' of the game of life known as 'continuous change', you are able to watch and respond in ways that may help others out of their shocks and shakings! Your detachment defines your availability for others – another seeming paradox to our conditioned minds.

The WHEN and WHERE of Detachment

We often acknowledge the value of detachment and our intention to 'detach' when we say things like, "I just need to step away for a moment" or "I just need to center myself" or "I can sense there is something I need to let go of here".

In this, the final part of this chapter on attachment/detachment, we explore the 'inner shift' that allows us to 'let go' and the various ways we can help our self to detach in different situations, thereby restoring our inner peace and inner power.

The shift from attachment to detachment or non-attachment is, in essence, a 'change of relationship'. To 'detach' is to change your relationship with the object of attachment.

Even though you may intellectually understand and acknowledge that 'nothing is mine' in absolute terms, the conditioning that plants the 'belief' in possessor/possessions is so deep that making this inner shift takes practice. Until, that is, you realize your true nature, at which point being non-attached is also realized to be your most natural state. In the meantime, you'll notice that when you consciously remind your self that nothing and no one is mine, you start to restore a deepening sense of freedom on the inside. This enables you to live with greater lightness and ease from inside out.

Here are seven ways that may help you to 'detach', if not a lot at first, then a little at least, in a variety of situations. Then little by little you will find your self feeling freer and therefore naturally happier.

Remember, attachment is all in the mind. It 'happens' in your mind. So detachment also 'happens' in the mind.

1 Change your relationship from possessor to trustee

Use when you get too attached to your possessions. Remind yourself nothing actually belongs to you. From the highest perspective, which is the spiritual perspective, you cannot own anything. However, you are a 'trustee' of every 'thing' in your life, until the time comes for someone else to have 'it' in their life! Often we have little or no say when that will be.

2 Let go

Use when you are holding on to a specific opinion/position. Next time you find yourself in an argument disarm the other by simply saying, "I don't agree with you but I accept that is your point of view. Tell me more so that I may understand why you see it that way". Remind your self that everyone has a different point of view because everyone is viewing from a different point.

So no one is right and no one is wrong in the universe of consciousness. There are just varying degrees of accuracy and varying degrees of ability to articulate that accuracy. Trying to be right and prove ourselves right is one of our most popular happiness killers!

3 Practise Giving

Use when you recognize yourself to be always wanting/desiring something from others. When you want something you are already attached to the object of your desire (including certain behaviors that we 'want' from others). Where? In your mind. Almost all of us learn this habit from not long after the moment we are born. This habit can be weakened and eventually broken by consciously practicing 'giving', free of any desire for anything in return. Giving what? Anything - time, energy, money, things, help, advice. The habit of wanting and taking is then gradually undone. Until that is, you realize you don't need anything from anyone beyond what you buy in a supermarket! That's where you fulfill your body's needs, but not your needs! When you start giving of your self an Aha! moment is likely to occur that reminds you that YOU have no need to acquire anything.

4 Mentally Rehearse Different Outcomes

Use when you are fearful of change and you are 'attached to' and 'comfortable with' the way things are. Or when you are holding on to some form of self-limitation (e.g. thinking 'I can't'). All the top performers in most sports now realize the power that comes from mental rehearsal or visualization.

Take a few minutes to visualize future changes as a preparation to accept and embrace those changes if and when they do arrive. 'See' yourself doing what you previously thought you couldn't. As you mentally practise you will find that you naturally start to 'let go' of the 'image/s' of the way things are and the 'idea' that 'I can't cope'.

5 Don't Identify with the Situation/Outcome

Use in any process, anytime and anywhere in life. This simply means don't make your happiness dependent on something outside your self, especially the results of your or other's actions. Don't wait to achieve some goal before you give your self permission to be happy (contented). Be contented whatever is the outcome of anything.

Happiness can be a choice and a decision, not a random experience or a dependency. Do something good, and in the 'process' of the doing of the good, you will notice happiness arising naturally 'during' the process and not just at the end. If it doesn't then you probably need to review your definition of 'doing good'. It's not the opposite of bad!

6 How Would Someone else Deal with the Situation

Use when your attachment to something or someone is obviously 'influencing' your ability to interact calmly and clearly with others. Take a moment to imagine how someone whose wisdom you respect would handle the situation. Perhaps a wise old uncle or aunt. This loosens your mental grip on 'your way' and weakens your habits of emotional reaction. If they are nearby ask them how they would respond. The conversation alone will allow a more detached perspective to crystalize within your consciousness.

7 Look at the Situation Through the Eyes of the Other Party

This is appropriate in all difficult relationships – this forces you to mentally release your attachment to one point of view and to generate understanding and empathy. Ask, listen, ask, listen, ask, listen, is the secret to understanding the others point of view. As you do you will see through the eyes of the other and free yourself in the process. They too are then more likely to realize their fixation on 'my way' and become more amenable to 'other' ways. It's no accident that the aspiration towards this kind of mutual understanding underpins most conflict resolution processes.

If you do decide to practise and experiment with any of the above it's perhaps best NOT to mention that you are doing so! Until the 'other' clearly understands the true meaning of detachment i.e. that it does not mean you do not care or that you are avoiding, there is a good chance they may find your intention either threatening or confusing.

Mums the word...as they say in some parts!

The WISDOM of Reflection

I am not saying you 'shouldn't' be attached or that it's 'bad' to be attached. But I understand it's easy to interpret everything here in that way. We all create attachments. Most of us believe that is the natural thing to do. So, when someone comes along and says things like all your stress, sorrow and suffering arise from you being attached to something or someone, many immediately want to resist that very idea. Maybe even throw the book in the bin!

All I am doing here is sharing some insights into the mechanics and implications of attachment. The intention is to help you look and see for your self. Then you decide whether you want to act on what you see.

Here are some practical ways that may help that process along. The following exercises and reflections may help you become more aware of what your specific attachments are and their effect in your day-to-day life. That awareness may (or may not) influence your relationship with your attachments e.g. loosen the attachment, a little ...gradually! Maybe!

II

AWARENESS
PAUSE

1 Write down all the things you are attached to, both the tangible (people and things 'out there') and the intangible (the ideas, beliefs and memories you are holding onto 'in here').

2 On a scale of one to ten rate each one for level of attachment - (1 is not very attached and 10 is extremely attached)

3 Write down the level of anxiety you have around the idea of losing each one - 1 is never any anxiety and 10 is incredibly anxious

4 How long do you think it would take you to recover if you lost each one - write down a time against each one e.g. an hour, or 2 days or perhaps 2 years etc.

5 What are the two main stories that you are currently creating in your mind and then losing your self in?

6 Which of the above strategies could you use immediately and in which situation?

7 Take a moment and 'reflect' on why love is not attachment - how would you explain that to someone?

8 Consciously practice the awareness of the 'detached observer' while watching a movie in the cinema or on TV, then do the same as you watch your version of the movie on the screen of your mind.

8

The Wisdom of
CONFLICT DISSOLUTION

**"To practice the process of conflict resolution it's necessary to
abandon the goal of getting people to do what we want"**
Marshall B Rosenberg

The Popularity of Conflicted Relationships

It's not hard to notice that life in almost all corners of the world
currently appears to be ravaged by conflict. Many people are habitually
quick to be in conflict with anything or anyone that seems to be in their
way. Some of the many also appear to go deliberately looking for
something or someone to be in their way! And as we know there are a
few whose life is dedicated to the violence of political and religious
conflict.

Others however, say there is now much less conflict in the world as
they cite the histories of world wars and the invading armies of cruel
empires. Then there are a few who say that most conflict today occurs
at a different, more personal, level. While there are many disputes over
land and legislation, over rights and resources, they say the conflicts of
modern times are more interpersonal than international, more internal
than external.

Whatever the truth about the scale and quantity of conflict one
condition remains the same; in any conflicted relationship, it always
takes 'two to tango'. There are always two parties/people involved in an
unhappy exchange of energy at some level.

When we are in the middle of any conflict it is hard to see and understand the true causes and dynamics of the dispute. The arising emotions are both distracting and blinding. Yet the causes of any conflict are usually closer to home than we think. Here are seven key 'insights' about the dynamics and characteristics of all conflicts at all levels. They may help you to walk your own path out of a difficult relationship and into liberation from mutually assured suffering.

INSIGHT 1

Your responsibility within any conflict situation in which you are involved is your contribution to the conflict.

The process of responding to any person or situation is something that happens within you. No one can make you perceive, think or feel anything without your permission. You are the creator. If you have been in conflict with someone for some time you are likely to be creating fear or anger towards them, and therefore expressing aggressive or passive aggressive behaviours or tendencies as you engage with them. As we explored earlier, the other person is not responsible for your emotions or your behaviours.

Your experience of the cycle of the conflict and your contribution to the conflict begins within your consciousness and is sustained within your consciousness. It begins with your perception of the other. If you perceive them darkly you will think darkly, feel dark, create a dark attitude, and behave darkly, thereby giving them dark energy. (see boxed text on next page) You don't have to. Perception is a choice and the clarity of that choice depends on how awake and aware you are. In essence, the dynamic of the conflict and the way out of the conflict looks like this:

When there is conflict there is mental/emotional pain. Yes?

Who creates your (mental/emotional) pain? You do!

Who creates at least half of the conflict? You do!

Who has the power to dissolve at least half the conflict? You do!

Where do you dissolve it?

Within your consciousness.

Within your self.

SOLUTION

First Dissolution then Resolution

When seen in this light, liberation from conflict is simply a decision. At any moment you can decide not to be in conflict! This is why all conflict resolution can only begin with 'conflict dissolution'. One party has to dissolve their contribution to the conflict, even if it is only temporarily, so that the process of resolution, which is another word for communication, can begin.

INSIGHT 2

The quality of energy you put into the conflict is likely to be the quality of energy you will get back.

What you give you receive, and what you receive is 'generally' the return of what you have already given. This is known as the Law of Reciprocity. Sometimes we call it sowing and reaping. Or for every action there is an equal and opposite reaction. Or cause and effect. Or what goes around comes around. In the East they sometimes call it 'karma'!

This one law and its many principles are what shape almost all relationships in the world. When

> ## Dark not Negative
>
> Notice I use the word 'dark' where most would probably use the word 'negative'. But there is no such thing as a negative or positive thought. Thoughts are created in consciousness and there is no duality in consciousness.
>
> There is only that which is aligned and emanating from your true nature, which is pure awareness, and that which is either a little unaligned or a lot unaligned.
>
> The extent of any unalignment is ultimately immeasurable, so it's what I call 'dark'. And just like the dying of the light at the end of each day there are varying degrees of darkness that would describe the energy of our consciousness in any conflict.
>
> It's simply a vibration of your consciousness, of you, that is not as natural or as pure as it could be!

you become aware of this law you become much more careful about the quality of energy you give to others, regardless of who they are or the situation you share with them.

Drop a stone in the water and the ripples it creates will reflect off any boulder in the pond and return to the point of origin of the ripple.

So too we 'drop in' to the great pond of life to create our journey in the context of our relationships. We are each walking radiators. At the subtlest level we radiate the ripples of attitude, and at the most gross level we radiate ripples of behaviour. Either way, what ripples out from us will likely return in a similar form/vibration.

Unless of course 'the other' is slightly more enlightened and they decide not to reflect the same dark energy but to return instead a more enlightened attitude and proactive behaviour. In which case, in that moment, they would be called 'a leader'. We are each capable of doing precisely that.

So if you are in a conflicted relationship it's useful to reflect on why you are receiving this dark energy from the other. Could it be because you gave them the same kind of energy sometime in the past day/week/month/year?

Are you caught in a seemingly perpetual exchange of darkness? If so who will be the one to break the cycle? Who will be more enlightened? Who will be the leader?

SOLUTION

The Shift from Wanting to Giving

Most conflicts are based in two parties both believing 'I am not getting what I want'. The thought process sounds like, "You are not doing what I want, you are not giving me what I want, you are not being the way I want you to be". Ultimately the most effective and fastest way to resolution is to stop wanting and start giving. This change of mindset sounds like, "What do you need, how can I help you, tell me what you want and let's see if I am able to give you that". Yes, it sounds like an idealistic and easy theory. And no, it's definitely not an easy mindset to adopt when in the middle of any heated exchange, especially if there's a history. But if practised in the lesser conflicts at first, eventually it's a wisdom that spills into the bigger ones.

INSIGHT 3

You cannot make anyone do or be anything because you cannot control another human being

In seeking the root cause of how and why we disempower our self so frequently in our relationships, we will always arrive at our belief system/s. We have all assimilated a number of common beliefs through childhood, education and cultural influences. Perhaps the most pervasive of these beliefs is around the issue of 'control'.

Almost every time you feel stressed or feel powerless or feel like a victim, it's usually because you are not able to do what you subconsciously believe you can and should be doing, which is to control others. It's accompanied by the, "I'm not getting what I want", thought!

Driving your controlling behaviour is the idea (another belief) that others are responsible for your happiness. This is easy to disprove when we watch two people responding to the same sporting event. One is celebrating and the other is upset and miserable. It's not the event that makes them feel happy or grumpy, it's what they do with the event in their consciousness, usually according to their beliefs

SOLUTION

The Shift from Control to Influence

While you cannot control others you can influence others. If you are a parent, a manager or anyone dealing with people as part of your role, it is your job to influence. How do you influence another person? There are a many ways such as respecting, listening, trusting, empathizing, encouragement, nurturing, suggesting etc. But the question is always what is the most effective way for this person, in this situation, at this moment.

This means you will need to fine tune your awareness and be creative. But you can't be sensitively aware and be consciously creative if you are upset, frustrated or grumpy in any way. That's why every relationship is an opportunity to exercise your creativity and to notice what you are placing in the way of your creative capacity within your self.

How do you know the difference between influence and control? If someone does not do what they said they would and you become upset it means you are trying to control. But if you have fully realized you cannot control anyone, ever, then you will never be upset with anyone, but you will ask why. You will seek to understand the other so that you can help them the next time.

INSIGHT 4

The resolution of all conflict begins at the mental level when you accept the other as they are in the moment.

Conflict shows up as behaviours expressing mutual resistance. When you resist anyone you are sending the 3C signal - you are CLOSED, giving birth to CONFLICT and trying to CONTROL. Your energy will take the emotional forms of fear or anger, perhaps a combination of the two, and you will be stressed. All created by YOU. There is only one shift to make if you want to stop making your self unhappy. That is into acceptance.

SOLUTION

The Shift from Resistance to Acceptance

When you move into acceptance you move from closed to OPEN, from control to INFLUENCE from conflict to RESOLUTION. Notice your energy is then calm and you are relaxed.

If you ever want to mentally and emotionally disarm another person in a conflict situation simply accept them as they are and their position/opinion as it is. It does not mean you agree – acceptance is not agreement. It doesn't mean you condone what they have said or done. It does mean you stop trying to make them as right as you believe you are! It does mean you can begin to communicate and begin to 'bring' them with you (or go with them) on the journey towards a mutually agreed solution. It's perhaps just a question of who will lead the way.

Acceptance is not the only step, just the first step. By accepting the other, as they are, by acknowledging and appreciating the others point of view, without judgment, you build trust and respect into the relationship. Only when respect is present is a real relationship possible. Unfortunately, we are mostly taught that the withdrawal of our respect for another is not only acceptable but often to be applauded. Much of the entertainment we consume is based on people justifying their disrespect towards others. Which goes a long way to explaining why the world of our personal relationships can be challenging and why the world of international relationships often seems to be filled with ...war.

INSIGHT 5

You are mentally attached to an outcome that is not happening in the physical dimension – only detachment can help you.

In all your conflicts you have an image in your mind of the result that you want – it may be something to do with a situation or a behaviour that you want from another. It's not happening in the physical dimension, so you are not getting what YOU want! If you didn't want a specific outcome there would not be a conflict. You would be open to the other party and curious to understand their point of view. The conflict is happening because of your attachment to that specific result and the method you are using to create the result is the least effective method. It doesn't matter how right or correct or accurate you 'believe' the outcome that you want may be.

SOLUTION

The Shift from Attachment to Detachment

Are you making your happiness dependent on the others behaviour or perhaps on the achievement of the outcome that YOU want? Do you believe (fear) that if you don't get the outcome you want your happiness/satisfaction will have been denied or sabotaged by the other? This is a common underlying fear that many carry into their relationships be they formal or informal. It sits at the root of most conflicts.

But now you know your happiness is not dependent on anyone or anything, yes? You now know that when your happiness disappears it's being denied/destroyed entirely by your self, by your 'attachment' to the outcome you want ...yes?

You also now know that if you believe it is being denied by 'them' you will blame them, project your pain (anger) on to them, play the role of victim and then try to defeat them in order to become victorious and thereby achieve your desired outcome...don't you? You can now see that in order to get what you want you then try to control the other, first in your mind, then with your words and then with your behaviour, am I correct? In an organization or even a family you are now aware that ultimately this will end in failure...aren't you?

Unless of course you pull rank. But if you pull rank you know you will eventually lose the trust, respect and the commitment of other/s, ...don't you? Pulling rank in the office or in the lounge is just the 'lazy mans' way to get what they want ...isn't it? When you are attached to a specific outcome, attached to the belief that the other has to change, that's what keeps you closed to other options, closed to other possibilities, closed to new ways forward. It shuts down your creativity and your ability to work with the other to find solutions. Before you can dissolve and resolve a conflict there has to be some level of detachment. (see The Wisdom of Detachment)

INSIGHT 6

All conflict is a cry for love.

Yes, even grown ups and seemingly well-loved people find themselves in conflicts in which they are hurting on the inside. They want something, some outcome, which they believe will satisfy them. But what they really want, deep down, even though they don't, won't or can't admit it, is love. It sounds trite and even dismissive of the validity of a conflict. However, next time you are in a conflict with someone ask your self how you would feel the moment 'they' say things like, "I appreciate you, I care about you, I want to understand YOU, I value you're input". Something melts?

SOLUTION

The Shift from Fear to Love.

If you are actively sustaining the conflict it means you are in a state of fear. It does not matter how right you are or even how happy you convince your self you are, to be so right! You are transmitting fear to the other while feeling fear-full within your self and thereby making your self unhappy. Perhaps this is the only solution - give love not fear. Obvious ...isn't it!

INSIGHT 7

When there are three parties involved in any conflict it probably means you are all stuck in some form of Karpman triangle.

If there are three of you and the conflict seems to be literally going round in circles it's probably because you are unwittingly playing the Drama Triangle Game. This is where each party interchanges with other the three roles that comprise the triangle - Persecutor, Victim and Rescuer.

It means all three are attached to certain outcomes at different stages of the interpersonal interactions within the threesome. They just get busy interfering with each other and then swap roles. It's one of the ego's most entertaining yet unhappy pastimes.

SOLUTION

Ask Google to enlighten you as to how The Karpman Drama Triangle works.

Seven Ways to use Detachment to Resolve Conflict

All conflict is based on two sides where each side is attached to something. The best application of detachment depends on the type of conflict as follows:

Method of Detachment	Best Time to Use
1 **Change your relationship from possessor to trustee**	When you notice you are too attached to your possessions
2 **Let go**	When you are holding on to a specific opinion/position
3 **Practice giving**	When you recognize yourself to be always wanting/desiring something from others
4 **Mentally rehearse different outcomes**	When you are scared of change or success
5 **Don't identify with the situation/outcome**	Appropriate in any conflict situation but you'll likely need a deeper level of self awareness to see it
6 **Imagine someone else dealing with the situation – how would they deal with it**	When your attachment is obviously influencing your ability to interact calmly with others.
7 **Look at the situation through the eyes of the other party**	Appropriate in all conflict situations –this mentally releases your attachment to one point of view and generates understanding of the other and empathy towards the other

The Seven Types of Conflict

There are basically seven types of conflict. Each one is based on the attachment to something in our minds. Resolution of each can only happen with the intention to let go of that 'something'.

See if you recognize any of these in your life, then identify what you are attached to and then what might be the most appropriate method to move towards resolution (previous page).

Type of Conflict	Example	What is the Attachment ?	How would You Resolve?
1 Disagreement	The dinner party argument: "I think the M25 should have 10 lanes. Your wrong, six lanes is enough! No it's not! Yes it is! No it's not! Yes it is!"	To an opinion	Agree to disagree
2 Misunder- standing			
3 Blame for the Past			

Type of Conflict	Example	What is the attachment?	How Would You Resolve?
4 Personality Clash			
5 Resistance to Authority			
6 Unmet Expectations of Another			
7 Position, Power or Privileges are Perceived to be Threatened			

Examples of 'possible solutions' to each are at the back of the book

When no one wants to let go!

If neither side is willing to let go and dissolve their contribution to the conflict, in order for the journey to resolution to begin, it's necessary to enter into a more formal approach known as Co-operative Resolution. It's a logical process that benefits from the presence of a facilitator or mediator.

The 7 steps are as follows.

1 Eliminate false conflicts i.e. disagreements, blame for the past and personality clashes

2 Clarify positions (what each side wants) and interests (why they want it).

3 Focus on common interests

4 Co-create possible solutions and then eliminate the impractical

5 Reach an agreement

6 Make a plan

7 Keep old perceptions and attitudes in check during the process.

There are numerous approaches to Conflict Resolution out there in the big wide world. Many are well refined and extremely sophisticated. But the basic cause of ALL conflict remains the same in EVERY instance. Attachment! But it seems few realize that ANY and ALL attachment leads to conflicted relationships and self-created suffering.

How are YOUR Difficult Conversations?

Conflicted relationships usually mean difficult conversations. Sometimes just changing the nature of the conversation can ease you out of conflict. Time spent focusing on enhancing the conversational dynamics can help the relationship be a little less ...difficult.

"How dare they speak to me like that!" is a thought that becomes a memory of a 'bad feeling'. That feeling becomes a fear that it may happen again. That fear becomes a mental and emotional obstacle that almost ensures you will have a difficult conversation in the future!

It seems that some people breeze through life without any problem when speaking to anyone and everyone. They cruise through all kinds of interactions while being open and reasonable, an empathic listener and a calm speaker with a warm personality and an acceptance of everyone - without having been anywhere near the Diplomatic Corp! While down at the other end of the conversational spectrum there are those who 'go off' like a box of fireworks in almost every encounter in which there is the slightest interpersonal sparkiness!

Most of us are probably somewhere in between. We are the 'inbetweeners', which means there are probably two or three people in our life with whom we just don't like to talk. However, like Olympic Diving, there are usually 'degrees of difficulty' which, in the context of a conversation can range from slightly awkward to extremely difficult to almost impossible.

The three main factors that underpin a difficult conversation are usually context, history and expectation.

Context usually means a conversation that is affected by perceptions of status and authority. It happens often between manager and staff, or parent and child, senior and junior. These tend to be two 'positions' talking **at** each other as opposed to two 'people' talking **with** each other. Not a good start. And unless one of the two can transcend their 'position consciousness' and connect with the other as a human being, it's likely to continue badly, as many managers and parents will testify!

History usually means the conversation is going to be awkward and difficult today, because there was a previous encounter, which was not pleasant, and it's still a fresh memory, from yesterday. It's not easy to meet 'the other' with a clean slate every time, let alone any time! Some things are hard to forget, including some conversations, especially if you see each other every day. But a 'clean slate' is such an ideal that is worth pursuing and a practice worth ...practising! Otherwise we bring our baggage to our difficult relationships. It weighs us down and it stifles and smothers the relationship, while making the conversations defensive, closed and cautious.

Expectation is either about what we want from the other or how we would like them to behave. Expectation tends to be the most common mistake that we make within our relationships and therefore conversations. Expectation tends to be what quickly reduces a dialogue, where we are mutually exploring together, into a discussion, which is a just an exchange of different points of view, down into an argument about who is more right than the other.

The expectation is usually a thought that sits silently present in mind and sounds like 'I expect to be right on this and I expect you to acquiesce'. Any conversation that kicks off from any expectation is almost bound to hit the rocks at some stage. But it's not easy to enter any interaction without expectation, or at least without a 'dependency' on one's expectation being fulfilled.

So here are eight suggested guidelines to drive, hazard and fog free, down the conversational road. Their usefulness and application, their emphasis and effectiveness, will vary depending on who exactly is in front of you, or the context of your exchange, or the history you share or your mutual expectations of one another. It's these four underlying factors that ensure many relationships, and their conversations, are a bit 'messy'.

1 Remember your primary responsibility

After a lifetime of conditioning in which we learn to believe it's 'the other' that makes you feel what you feel, and therefore think what you think, and do what you do, it's not easy to remember ...no it's not them, it's me! Most conversations will drive up to this illusion and either get stuck, as the habits of emotional reaction and blame kicks in, or both parties will give up and back away with a simmering, mutual resentment. A conversation between two self made victims seldom goes very far. Don't wait for your post conversational personal reflections to realize that you reacted because you forgot to take responsibility for your own emotional state. Otherwise life becomes a series of very brief conversations!

2 Respect is the secret ingredient

Difficult conversations are often with a) someone of whom we are scared, which means we are fearful of what they might say or do, or b) with someone that we have decided we simply don't like. Any previous negative experiences i.e. memories of suffering that you attributed to them or any previous negative judgment, will not allow you to respect the other. You won't be able to affirm their innate worth and goodness as a human being. And any conversation that is without mutual respect to some degree or other is going to flounder as animosity flourishes.

If you cannot instantly rise above such memories/judgments, or put them to one side, try this interim measure to introduce respect from your side of the table. Find at least one or two positive qualities or attributes within 'the other' and see them as that during your interactions. You don't need to say what you see is good in them, although you can say it. Sometimes it helps. But primarily it's your vision of them that 'transmits' to them that you are ascribing value to something within them, however small. They will then sense that you value them.

This is sometimes enough to unblock your own ability to connect and communicate calmly and clearly, and it makes it easier for them to reciprocate by responding openly and proactively. But don't depend on it happening instantly!

3 Resistance only leads to persistence so ...stop it!

Once you have accepted that it's you that is responsible for what you feel it'll be easier to dissolve your resistance to 'them', even when you don't agree with their idea and/or their opinion. Resistance kills our capacity to hear the other clearly and eats away at our ability to understand them. Misinterpreting and misunderstanding are the most common ingredients of a difficult conversation. All because of mutual resistance.

Acceptance doesn't mean you agree but it does mean any disagreement ceases to be an obstacle to your connection and communication. Who stops resisting first? The one who decides to lead!

4 Listen from your heart as well as your head

Listening from the heart can instantly soften a difficult conversation and remove most of the difficulty. Instead of being concerned just with their facts and your feelings, you become equally interested in the feelings of the other. You are also ready and willing to share your own feelings when the moment is right. But in a way that isn't just dumping all your emotions onto them. Listening from the heart is a skill, an art, that some people seem to have naturally while others take a lifetime to learn.

It can be difficult for some to say what they feel as opposed to what they think, as many of us don't know the difference between our thoughts and feelings, most of the time. Start to practice expressing your feelings in quiet and humble ways, on your own, in front of a mirror, or in the car, as you talk to your self (when you're on your own of course!).

Once you start listening and speaking from the heart you start to create a deeper connection with the other. That's when all those ideas and opinions, memories and perceptions from the past, start to lose their power to make the conversation unpleasant.

5 Be like a bendy toy

When entering into a difficult conversation there is usually something that we want or something we don't want, which is also a want! This will always be a threat to your ability to stay calm, be flexible, to compromise, to roll with the others energy. This 'wanting' creates rigidity while diminishing your ability to understand the other. If there is one thing that is going to make a difficult conversation difficult it's mutually rigid misunderstanding based on what 'I want'.

But who is going to start being flexible...first? Who will offer to compromise...first? Who will enquire and acknowledge how the other 'feels'...first? Who will let go of their 'position'...first? Who will bend with the breeze, a little...first?

6 Avoid presumption, assumption and consumption

It almost goes without saying that conversations work better when we presume nothing and assume nothing. Most of us know the consequences of presumption and assumption and the time and energy it can take to repair a relationship that has gone askew because of either. When you make an assumption or presumption you become 'closed' around your own judgments and conclusions about their motivation, intention and behaviour. Being open, even when you want to be closed around your assumptions, is an obvious imperative to a stress free exchange. Otherwise it just gets very tense for both parties.

Even better is to genuinely care about the other. When you can care for and about the other you will do less 'telling' and more 'asking', which in turn will naturally reveal and dissolve your assumptions. Too much care however and you are likely to consume the others story and live their story as if it was your own, recreating their emotions as if they were your own. It's a fine line ...sometimes!

7 Drop the past and pick up the future

This is both an obvious and valued principle of all conflict resolution and all effective communication strategies - don't dwell in the past by continuously going over the past. Ask only once what happened and what, if anything, can we learn. Then, how do we go forward, how will we deal with the same situation/issue next time? Revisiting the past tends to generate emotional heat and the impulse to search for someone to project that heat on to. This is often why some conversations can easily descend into an emotional flame-throwing contest.

8 Never 'Dextify'

Watch out for the following symptoms from our old friend the ego! Defending, explaining and justifying - otherwise known as 'dextifying'! Not a good idea. As soon as you do you are saying, 'I am on the defensive' and the other may start to think they have power over you. And unless and until they realize it's an illusory power, they may just try to keep it up.

It's not easy to NOT jump into defending, justifying or explaining mode when challenged in any way. One thing that helps is to create the habit of asking before telling. By asking how they perceive or interpret the issue/situation/topic, you give your self the opportunity and space to restore your inner calm and openness. Then there is more likely to be a reciprocal response of, "Well what do YOU think, how do YOU see it?" In that moment all difficulty in the conversation tends to dissolve. You are chilled because you are no longer reactively 'dextifying'. And they are open.

Conversations become difficult for different reasons. But the root cause always lays within ones self, not them! It's really just a statement to our self that we need to learn more about our self and why we are making things difficult in the first place. But it's not easy to see that the other person is never the problem, regardless of what they say or do.

But if we can say to our self, 'now what is this person, this conversation, this scene we are both in, trying to teach me', we may find that we can come away from the interaction with some moments of personal enlightenment and access to a deeper strength within our self. It's just that we may have to do that in retrospect at first!

II

A W A R E N E S S
P A U S E

Questions

What are the conflicts you are involved in now? Make a list, regardless of how small.

What are you attached to in each of those conflicts?

Imagine each conflict is resolved. What does it look like and feel like?

What can you see your self doing in order to get there?

Reflection

Recall a conflicted relationship from the past that has since resolved so there is no longer a conflict. What were the main factors in its resolution?

Action

Identify the two people in your life with whom you tend to have difficult conversations. Which of the above strategies may help in each of those relationships?

Contemplation

"The first to apologize is the bravest
The first to forgive is the strongest
The first to forget is the happiest"
Anon

9

The Wisdom of
AWAKENING

> "Your vision will become clear when you look
> into your heart. Who looks outside dreams,
> who looks inside awakens"
> **Carl Jung**

So you think you're awake!

Well are you sure? When you sleep you dream. We all dream. Some remember their dreams. They even repeat the same dream. Others can't remember their dreams at all. Or, on awakening, they almost instantly forget. Many of us have probably dreamed a dream and while in the dream state believed we are fully awake and that 'this is real'.

Have you ever had such a dream? You dreamed in such a way that the dream is so clear, so vivid, the images and the feelings seemed so like real life? Then suddenly you awaken and only then do you realize you were asleep and dreaming. You awaken to reality.

But is it the ultimate reality?

At this moment it is probably fairly certain that you're not having one of those lucid dream moments. Yes? Well it turns out you probably are, in a funny sort of way. You are in a kind of waking dream and you're not aware of it. And like the 'sleeping dream' you are not aware you're asleep and dreaming until you wake up.

So how exactly are you dreaming the world and how do you wake your self up? At every moment we are creating our own 'versions' of the world and the people around us, and then giving the status of reality to our 'versions' of it/them.

The key word is 'reality'. You believe what you see is real but, in actuality, it's not as real as it could be. Let's say I was sitting in front of you now. I would probably not be as real as I could be ...in your reality. Your reality is not out here where I am sitting. It's in your consciousness. That's where you create your version of reality, your version of me, and that's why it's unique to you. That's why no one shares the same reality.

Have you ever gone to see a movie with a friend then, as you talked about it afterwards, you suddenly found you saw different things or have completely different interpretations of the same scene or character? Sometimes you just can't remember seeing some of the things the other saw and vice versa. Were you watching the same movie? Yes, but each creates their own version of the movie in their consciousness.

Before we investigate further and understand the exact nature of our 'sleepy dream', even while we are apparently awake, there are three words that will recur in the following exploration and unfolding of our understanding - belief, version and reality.

Belief - is what you think is true but don't know is true, but you don't want to say, "I don't know"!

Version - is your unique creation of everything and everyone, shaped by your belief/s, within your consciousness.

Reality - is the true reality, unbiased and undistorted by any belief or memory.

The classic example of the undoing of the 'waking dream', in order to reveal reality, is of course the story of The Emperor's Clothes. Everyone agrees to believe the Emperor is wearing beautiful clothes, so each person creates their own version of a beautifully dressed emperor in their consciousness. Everyone agrees the Emperor is beautifully dressed. Until, one day, someone, let's call them the 'waker upper', (an innocent child) breaks the spell, says it like it is, thereby triggering the awakening of everyone as they start to see and acknowledge reality. The emperor is in fact completely naked.

Right now I'm playing the role of 'waker upper', so to speak. Then, when you feel sufficiently awake your self, you can do the same for others.

But before we dig down deep in our consciousness, in order to prod or tickle ourselves awake, let me share a couple of examples of sleepiness and dreaminess from the apparent realities of day-to-day life.

Someone Else's Version

I'm sure you've experienced the following in some way or other. You are about to meet someone for the first time but before you do a friend tells you how awful they are, perhaps how devious they are, or how negative they are and how grumpy they always are. So you 'believe' your friends version of them. Notice, when you do meet that person that's exactly what you see in them, or near enough. It's what you expect. Your version of them is shaped by the assimilated beliefs about them that you heard from your friend.

But then, as the encounter progresses, you slowly but surely start to see they are not at all the way your friend described. In fact, they are calm, open and positive, and you quite enjoy their company. In other words, you awaken to another reality as you create your own version of them based on your direct experience of them. You awaken from a dream that you have created using your interpretation of another's ideas and beliefs about them.

Your Version of Another

Then there's that person whom you did meet and you decided, "What an idiot, what a fool, I felt really hurt when they called me silly". You leave the encounter with a set of beliefs such as, "He's an idiot and he hurt my feelings". So your version of them is shaped by your created beliefs following a direct encounter with them. Three days later you see them, recognize them, and walk up to speak to them. But you don't seem to connect very well.

In fact, every time you meet that person there seems to be a lack of genuine 'connection'. The conversation is awkward and nothing seems to flow. You put that down to confirmation of your beliefs about them i.e. your version of them that you created some days ago. You may even think quietly, "I knew I was right about them!". Your inability to 'relate' well was obviously hampered by the memory of your hurt feelings that you attributed to them.

What you don't realize is you weren't connecting with them or relating to them, you were connecting with, and relating to, your beliefs about them, within your memorized version of them. You were in your own dream state and they (your version of them) were at the center of your dream.

Liberating Insights

But then off you go on your 'spiritual self-awareness' course where you learn two things common to most self-awareness workshops, seminars and courses these days. One, everyone is innately good at heart and when you see that goodness in the other it not only brings goodness out in you it brings it out in them. It's an insight that seems intuitively accurate. And two, no one else is responsible for what you feel. That's your job, so to speak! Suddenly these two insights/realizations completely change the way you create your version of that person.

You confirm this the next time you meet. You see them as an intrinsically good person despite their attitude or behaviours. And you no longer believe they can hurt your feelings. You notice the exchange is much smoother, not perfect as it takes a little time to completely free your consciousness of the old version. But it feels like there is a truer, cleaner connection.

So your beliefs were shattered and a deeper truth allowed you to create a different version of them and it felt like you were 'waking up' to a new reality in that relationship.

Now You

Now, it's obviously up to you to see which beliefs you may need to release so that you can stop dreaming, so that you can see a deeper truth and thereby 'awaken' to a new, more accurate reality.

Before you take that deeper dive into 'awakening from the dream' there is one rather useful question, which is *how do you validate you have awoken and you are creating a truer reality*? Answer: There will be a gradual, sometimes instant, disappearance of suffering. Not pain but suffering.

Your Perception is Your Reality

There's an old but now well quoted saying that goes something like this: "I know I do not see the world as it is, I see the world as I am". This is the idea that your perception and interpretation of people and the world around you is shaped by how you see your self.

The implication being that if you do not know and see your self accurately you will create a distorted perception, an unreal version, of events and people around you.

If you believe you are an architect then you will drive through a city and your perception will likely focus primarily on the buildings and the quality of architecture of the city. You will evaluate and hold that city in your consciousness according to your 'created' perceptions/evaluations of building design. For most other people it's just a bunch of buildings and just another city.

If you believe you are a shopkeeper (because you own a retail shop) every time you enter other shops you will likely assess many attributes like layout, easy movement of customer traffic, product displays etc. For everyone else it's just another shop.

If you believe you are a supporter of a certain team then supporters of other teams will be seen as 'different', perhaps not quite so welcome, perhaps the enemy! Those that don't support and identify themselves with a specific team just enjoy the game.

Little do we realize we use our beliefs to create a form of limitation in our consciousness. We limit our self, according to what we believe our self to be. Yet the architect is not an architect, it's what they do, not what they are. The shopkeeper is not a shopkeeper, it's what they do, not what they are. The team supporter is not the team, but so strongly is he identified with the team he almost believes he is!

Then we filter and interpret the world according to how we see our self. It's just something we learn and develop. It's not wrong, just inaccurate. It's not bad, it's just that our beliefs cloud our clarity and it's as if we are creating our own dream version of the world accordingly, without being aware we do so. It's often quite subtle.

It's our beliefs that shape our perceptions. Together they form our versions of reality. That's the bit no one teaches us as we grow up.

Our beliefs and perceptions filter reality into a waking dream. If that idea or insight is just a bridge too far, consider the following examples of common beliefs that ensure we stay asleep to reality, unaware of the truth i.e. the true reality.

We all know that other old, but profound saying, 'the truth will set you free', which is another way of saying the 'realization of what is true will wake you up'.

See if the following examples resonate with you.

1 Are you unworthy?

This habitual, 'I am unworthy' belief, about the 'self', will suppress both your intelligence and your potential.

It's not uncommon to BELIEVE "I am not worthy... of the job...of the relationship...of happiness". It's usually a belief we learn to form at a young age when our parents project their sense of unworthiness on to us. It easily becomes a subconscious belief that may rule our entire life.

It means we will regard our self as 'inferior' and of much lesser importance than others. We will elevate others in our own minds, usually way to high, probably way beyond how they even regard themselves. We may even project such greatness on to some others that we will keep our self at a distance as we feel we are not worthy to be in their company, for more than a few moments.

Our belief in our unworthiness will shape then our relationships and therefore our life, possibly without us realizing. Little do we know that the truth is every human being is of equal worth. Why? Because every human being is a source of the most valuable (worthwhile) energy in human life, and that is love.

Everyone can give love and that's what everyone tends to value most, knowing or unknowingly. And that's why we are each as valuable as the next person despite status, reputation, appearance or wealth.

Undoing the habit of believing in our illusory unworthiness does wonders for our wellbeing.

2 Are you a people pleaser?

This habit will not allow you to develop respect for others.

Are you subtly or not so subtly looking for the approval of others because you BELIEVE you must please others or another?   And when you fail, when you don't manage to 'apparently' please another what do you feel? Perhaps sad, maybe irritated, angry? At them, or at your self?

But perhaps the truth is you cannot please anyone simply because everyone pleases themselves. Proof? Today I give a chocolate cake and of course you seemed pleased. Tomorrow I give you the same chocolate cake but this time you grumpily say, "Not chocolate cake again"?

If you go through life 'believing' you have to please others and thereby gain their approval then you'll likely create many scenes in your waking dream in which you will make your self unhappy! Some even say that any unhappiness is a sign you are creating and living in unreality! The truth maybe as simple as - each and every one of us pleases our self, or not, as the case may be!

3 Are you a victim?

This habitual belief will not allow you to develop the art of empowering your self and being an inspirations for others. Undoing it releases your natural power.

Perhaps the most popular dream state is when you BELIEVE your self to be on the end of something 'bad'. Many conversations are filled with, "Can I tell you what just happened to me"?   Followed by, "Do you know how that made me feel".

The arrival of the electricity bill, the weather forecast for the day, our child's decision to stay in bed, the missing item at the supermarket, the list of things that happen that we then take personally, is perhaps rather endless. It is of course different things for different people.

So here is another old saying that may contain a truth that will set you free of the habit of making your self a victim; 'nothing happens *to* me, everything happens *for* me'. Change one two-letter word and suddenly you are a master. But please do not believe me, try it and see. It's a different way to perceive events. Some say it's a truer way, a way to awaken from that waking dream and restore your awareness of true reality.

4 Are you a worrier?

This habit will not allow you to develop your capacity to be loving and caring towards others. Undoing it will also stop you wasting time and energy.

Most mothers are world champion worriers. Many of us seem to enjoy our daily 'worry session'. Even if just quietly, with a coffee of course! It's a habit where we BELIEVE something awful is going to happen. Sometimes we completely misuse our imagination and visualize catastrophe. At other times it's just nagging little thoughts that something bad is about to happen.

The worry thoughts ensure we filter the world around us for threats that may fulfill our catastrophic prophesies. We perceive people and events as possible portents that something is going to go wrong in our life. Then we keep rerunning our worry stories, occasionally alongside a big loud voice in our head shouting 'I told you so'.

And then when someone says, "There's nothing to worry about" we either reply, "Oh yes there is", or we are quietly thinking, "Little do they know".

How much of our life is spent watching movies? Probably weeks, maybe months, for some, maybe even years. How much of our life do we spend activating the BELIEF that something could, is, will, go horribly wrong? Only when we notice that our fantasized catastrophizing is a complete waste of time and energy will we awaken from our worry dreams that are filled with anxiety and false foreboding. Only when we learn to quietly hold our attention on the moment, on the here and now, on being fully present, does the worry habit begin to atrophy, as we awaken from our long fretfully, dreamy slumber.

5 Have you 'fallen' in love?

This habit won't allow you to develop your authenticity and integrity. It's an illusion that requires unlearning if you want to know love, truly.

Perhaps the most powerful dream is based on the BELIEF in romantic love. We absorb so many tales when we are young that life will become somewhat magical when we find the perfect other and 'fall' in love. For many it shapes their entire life as they go searching for the love of another believing that love must be found and that it arrives from somewhere 'out there'. It's a powerful dream state!

A few awaken to the realization that love does not make you fall, it elevates, liberates and empowers. And it doesn't come from another, it is what we are in our highest state of consciousness. But this is a tough dream to awaken from as our illusions about love are so deeply embedded and, for some, their neediness is so great, they cannot imagine a happy life without that special other.

Yet, when the truth is seen or even glimpsed most of us recognize that love isn't another commodity to be acquired and used, it is the very nature of every individual human being. When you know that love is what you are, in essence, when you are fully awake and aware, then life suddenly reveals a new meaning and a powerful purpose. That revelation takes place entirely within your own consciousness.

But once again, don't believe me. Awaken and see for your self. Or perhaps that should read 'see for your self and awaken from the dream you didn't even know you were dreaming'!

These are but a few of many beliefs that we have assimilated and allowed to shape our perceptions as we create our own versions of reality that are not true.

Middle of the night sleeping dreams can be a bizarre mix of images and symbols. Sometimes we awaken in a confused and perplexed state asking what was that all about. Do you ever wonder why events happening in the world seem weird; why people around you seem unfathomable in their behaviours? The answer often has nothing to do with them, but all to do with the fact that you are in a dream state, unable to make coherent sense of such images, events and behaviors.

But we each have an alarm clock that reminds us that it's time to wake up and get up. It's called stress, sometimes known as confusion, often showing up as anger, fear, resentment, anxiety, depression, irritation, terror, frustration, panic, hopelessness, powerlessness. And a few more!

These emotions are the sounds of our alarm clock. Yet so many of us will reach inwards, turn it off, ignore its signal, turn over and go back to sleep!

II
A W A R E N E S S
P A U S E

Questions

What factors, other than your beliefs, shape the way you create
your version of someone in your consciousness?

What are the beliefs that you can now see are not allowing you
to perceive others with clarity?

Reflection:

Think of three people that you know, but find your self not liking
very much. Then apply the two insights above to your version
of them and see if it makes a difference to your attitude.

Action

Pick two stories from the news today and identify the beliefs
that people are holding that are distorting their perceptions and
not allowing them to see the 'reality' of the situation.

Experiment with two people you know this week by creating
a new version of each and then allowing that to shape
your behaviour towards them. Notice the effect on the relationship,
if any.

Contemplation

"If you change the way you look at things,
the things you look at change"
Dr Wayne Dyer

10

The Wisdom of
LIVING LIGHTLY

> "Soon silence will have passed into legend. Humanity has turned its back on silence. Day after day he invents machines and devices that increase noise and distract us from the essence of life, contemplation and meditation."
> **Marcel Marceau**

Where IN the World are YOU?

How do we live IN the world without being rocked, shocked or knocked BY the world? How can we live IN the world and give TO the world with generosity and gratitude, and not become agitated when it (they!) don't return the same? How can we walk gracefully through our life IN this world and remain free of all resentment or animosity towards anyone or anything that we may encounter on our way?

There are no easy answers to such questions because it seems we have all learned to make the same mistake. We tend to see the world out there as the only reality with little awareness or understanding of the universe within. As a consequence, we allow ourselves to be easily over powered BY the world. We become consumers OF the world. And then become addicted TO the world. As a result, we become almost totally dependent ON the world. Within the 'reality' of our consciousness that means we are no longer 'free spirits'. We have been captured BY the world, or, more accurately, we have used the world as an idea and set of images in which to lose our self!

And that's why we are so often not so happy within our self, why we become grumpy with each other and why our 'joie de vivre' is somewhat diminished!

Through the ages the solution offered by the sages and the saints, by the wisest elders and the most enlightened masters, has been simple. In a universal chorus across history almost all have recommended that we realise and remember one thing: you are IN this material world but you are not OF this material world! It's an insight that indicates a way of correcting our relationship WITH the world. Easy words but not so easy to realise and implement here ...IN this world!

Another way to articulate that insight might be: realize that you are a non-material being with a non-material identity, inhabiting a material form and living life in a material world. Realize that you are a being of consciousness first, with no worldly identity, and that you occupy a form comprised of the same physical elements as those of the physical world around you. Realize that you are 'the dweller' and your form is just a dwelling!

Our habit of making the world, and things in the world, more real and more important than our self is deep. We find it hard to let go of the tendency to make the world our 'only' source of security and happiness. We have forgotten the real meaning of 'be your self' as we use the things of the world to build many 'selves'. We find it difficult to 'switch off' our craving FOR the world and the things OF the world. So it becomes 'not so easy' to restore our sense of who I am.

And so we come full circle from Chapter 1 where we explored the insight that reminds us that any sense of identity based on anything IN this world is an illusion i.e. it's not true. This is the heart of personal undevelopment. Once realized it becomes obvious that no one 'develops' anything apart from physical skills or aptitudes. There is no need. The self is already fully and completely the self. It's just a question of how quickly and how efficiently we can each stop using the world and things in the world to create our many illusory senses of self.

It's a question of how easily you can undo the habits and tendencies, that you have created and engrained in your consciousness, based on those illusory selves, that stand in the way of being your true and authentic self.

Like the first flower on the cover of this book we strangle our self with a jungle of weeds of our own making. They are simply metaphors for the beliefs, memories, ideas, habits, tendencies and objects that we create and record within our self, and then attach our self to. Clearing the jungle is our only task. Unlearning and undoing is our task. Cultivating our own insight and wisdom and then applying it is our task. Allowing what is naturally already present within us, within the authentic you, to flower and express is the task.

But it's not just another task that has a beginning and an end with a timeline in between. This is the one task that in many ways is infinitely depthless, timeless and endless. As soon as you ask how long it may take it's already taking too long.

To assist you in the restoration of your true sense of 'who I am'; to help you reveal the attributes of your authentic self and thereby recover the mastery of your own inner universe of thought and feeling, vision and attitude; here are some insights and practices, some meditations and contemplations, that may help.

1 A Day Without Desires

The most frequent habitual thought form that we tend to create each day is probably 'desire'. It's those moments that we want something from the world. It sounds like, "I want more time ...I want a good job ...I want a nice partner ...I want a sunny holiday ...I want this to be over ...I want to be perfect"!

Desire always has an object. It is the grasping for the object at the mental level that keeps our consciousness agitated, anchored IN the world and therefore vulnerable TO the world. It is 'desire' that keeps our minds in a state of peacelesness and 'ever busy' with images and ideas of the world. The 'desire habit' causes us to lose our ability to focus for any length of time and eventually seems to drain our power.

Built into every desire is the fear that we will neither achieve nor acquire the object of our desire. That desire induced fear is one of our favourite forms of stress. Desire is also how we perpetually delay our happiness as we expect something IN the world will 'make' us happy at some time in the future. A future that often never arrives while the desire habit still lives.

As you practice a day without desire you will begin to notice just how many times and in how many ways 'desiring something' arises. And yet each time a desire arises it is an opportunity to let it pass and choose to be the master creator of your own contentment in this moment NOW! And when you do let it pass you feel a freedom from tension, albeit a subtle tension, on the inside. It's like an inner exam that you pass easily by ...letting it pass! It's also one of the signs that the journey back to mastery has begun!

2 The Art of Detached Involvement

Any form of attachment to anything IN the world must also bring fear. Fear of loss or damage. Each interaction and every relationship is an opportunity to practise the art of being detached but remaining involved. In so many of our conversations we hear the 'others story' about what happened to them. We absorb their judgments and their feelings. As we listen we allow our selves to be 'sucked in' to their story, identifying with their story, and recreating our version of their emotions and feelings within our self.

This keeps our consciousness agitated. We become busy imagining the scenes and circumstances of 'their' experiences in their world. As we become lost in a jungle of thoughts and feelings based on their story it feels like we have no control over our own 'insperience'.

The art of 'detached involvement' sounds like a contradiction but it's not. It is an art that allows us to hear the other, be present for the other, empathize with the other, but not waste our mental energy recreating the thoughts and feelings of the other. It means that while we acknowledge and understand the others story, and perhaps their suffering, we do not 're-live it' within our self.

This does not mean we don't care about the other. In fact, it enhances our ability to be caring. The less 'emotionally' involved we are the less busy we become with our own feelings, so the more we are available and able to be sensitive to their needs and meet their need to be fully heard in that moment.

3 Stillness in Motion

It has long been known that at the heart of the consciousness of every human being there is a place, an 'inner space', that never ever changes. It is this inner space that gives you your stability, your internal reference point, regardless of the chaos that may be happening around you. It is ultimately 'what' you are! But it's as if we lose our connection to it, our awareness of it, our ability to be 'in it'. But it's always there. Being the 'still point' is the foundation of your stability, while the world around you, near and far, can appear to be in chaos. Being the 'still point' is a practice that helps you to see the transience, the fleetingness, the impermanence, of everything in life, except your self. Viewing life from the 'still point' allows you to see life more as a process or flow, rather than a static set of circumstances in which you may also believe you are stuck.

Everything is energy, and energy is always changing its form, often flowing like a river into another state. As you watch all levels of change in the world can you 'allow' the river of life to flow round you and past you? Just 'watching' means you cease trying to stop it, block it, fix it or control it. As you 'let go' and watch the flow, you are like a rock in a river, strong and stable. The rock never interferes with the river, it worries not how the river has 'been' flowing or 'will' flow.

Yes, it's true, rocks don't act in the world and YOU do. So can YOU be still while moving, can YOU be still while acting, can YOU be still while thoughts are arising, can YOU be still while everything that is not you, including your thoughts and feelings, are in constant motion?

That is the daily practice on the way to mastery!

4 Observe from Above

Sometimes this is called 'helicoptering out'. It's that moment when you rise above the scene in front of you, 'as if' you are leaving your body 'down there' in the scene. But you, the being of consciousness, rise up and away. And as you rise 'above it all', your perspective changes. The scene you were involved in shrinks, not only in perspective, but also in significance, as you see a 'bigger picture'. And eventually, as you continue rising, even the bigger picture also becomes small and much less important. The difficult circumstances that felt like mountains really do start to appear as molehills.

And if you can rise above it all and pull your perspective far enough away, like astronauts on a journey away from the physical world, you will see that 'the all' and 'the everything' are merged in one tiny point in the distance. The insignificance of almost everything becomes apparent. Events and circumstance lose their effect upon you. You easily remain cool! You may even see and realise that every scene that appears in front of you is just a fleeting image in the larger drama, one small frame in the reel of the movie called life.

From this perspective of the ever-changing events and circumstances of the world, it becomes easier to diminish and eventually be free of your 'cravings' for the world to 'appear' as you want, exactly when you want, and give you what you want.

5 Vision of Oneness

The idea of interconnectedness is not new. Intellectually we can grasp how everything in the world is connected and therefore related. But it's not an easy vision or awareness to hold on a day-to-day and moment-to-moment basis. Some of our deepest mental habits are to separate and fragment, compartmentalise and label.

This keeps us stuck in the 'details' of the world. It keeps our nose up against the picture believing that the fragment that we see is quite separate from everything else, and that it is only this fragment that matters. A vision of oneness happens when your consciousness 'clicks' into an awareness that everything is interconnected, whole, complete ...one.

Can you see one world, can you perceive one family, can you sense just one (his) story that we ALL share together? This vision allows you to see everything that appears to be happening anywhere, at any time, like waves in the ocean.

Close or far, the many events and ever changing circumstances in the world are wavelike. They rise and fall, ebb and flow, and then merge back into the ocean of life's unending drama. The master is not disturbed by the sound, nor by the sight, nor by the effect, of any wave!

6 Listen to the Silence

Behind all creativity and prior to all creation is silence. The artist begins with a blank canvas ...silence. Between the notes of a symphony is nothing but ...silence. Between and behind your thoughts is the power of your being ...your silence. From the silence of the self comes all creation.

As long as you remain busy WITH the world, and occupied by all that appears to be happening IN the world, you will not see, hear or know the silent canvas on which all creation sits and from which all creation emerges.

As long as you remain busy with thoughts and ideas, memories and speculations, you will only live on the ever moving, thrashing, chaotic surface of life. You will miss the deep peace of that stillness, the immense beauty of the silence, that is not of this world.

As long as you are busy with the 'noise of change', as long as you stay busy being bewitched, often beguiled and sometimes bewildered, by the secondary reality of the world out there, you may never know the power and richness of your silent, inner state.

Take a moment to be otherworldly. Listen to the symphony of silence at the core of your being. It's not an escape, it's not a denial, nor an avoidance of the world. It is to bring your power and the beauty of your being, your creative genius, into the world. This is why the pastime of most masters is some way of meditation. Meditation takes you past the awareness of time and space, borders and boundaries. It takes you into the reality of the silence and stillness of your being, where time does not exist and space has no boundaries. It brings you home.

7 Imitate a Seed

Hold the seed of any plant in the palm of your hand and it seems so small and insignificant, so inert and static. And yet the complete blueprint of the future growth of its form, colour and fragrance, are merged within. It is the perfect metaphor for the 'light of consciousness', for the self that 'I am', that 'you are'. Real rest and renewal happens when you can bring your consciousness into a seed like state. When the 'I' that says 'I am' is in its 'seed state' input from the senses is temporarily suspended.

There is no sensual stimulation. The energy of the self is at rest. The mind is completely still without thought, the intellect is silent without evaluation or judgment. All the tendencies and traits of your personality have temporarily dissolved back into the light of you, so there are no cravings or impulses towards action. The conscience is still and the memory bank has been temporarily shut down. There is a complete and natural detachment from the material world.

In this state there is not even an awareness of self, no sense of I, simply complete and utter stillness. You are like the seed before it enters the soil and starts to germinate, grow and express. In that state you 'know' one thing; you are IN the world but not OF the world.

You don't 'think it. You just 'know it. But you don't live in this state while in the world. That's not the aim. But to occasionally taste this 'reality' is to restore your awareness of the primary reality within your self, and regain your mastery of your inner world.

From that state comes a very different way of living IN the big wide world around you.

Joining the Dots

Time management is attention management, which is self-management. Stress management is change management, which is response management, which is self-management. Conflict management is relationship management, which is attachment management, which is self-management. Emotion management is ego management, which is self-management.

Yes it's all about your 'self'! All roads lead back to YOU. But not in a narcissistic sense. It's about understanding and managing, sometimes creating and sometimes destroying, what is IN you so that you can be YOU and not the distorted version of you that you learned from others.

It's within you that all the topics we've covered are intimately connected. The seed of the need to manage any of them is our old friend the ego. If it was not for the ego you would be your natural self. And that's the only time you don't need to manage anything, inside or outside.

That's the time when you are transparent and calm in all situations as nothing can shake you. You stand in your power. That's when you are always warm and caring without needing to think or decide whether you should be warm and caring. It's always your most natural way to be and do. That's the time when you are happy and contented, without needing anything or anyone to induce your happiness or your contentedness. It arises naturally from the heart of your being.

Yes, that state of being exists within all of us right now. But just as the stone gathers moss as it rolls down the hill so we've all gathered our personal moss called beliefs, illusions, attachments, dependencies, habits of thought, and patterns of emotions. We have not only gathered but created all these inner companions that have kept us asleep, unaware and unwise, even in those moments when we 'thought' we were awake, aware and wise!

The process of undevelopment and unlearning is not defined by a timeline or by any particular technique. For some it seems to occur almost instantly and for others it seems to be a lifetime endeavour. There is no one methodology that gets you there faster. Only interest and curiosity, patience and persistence, the willingness to release and experiment, are all necessary 'inner conditions' that take you there. It's different ways for different people at different times, as we all make our way back to where we began. Bon voyage!

The Art of Detachment and the Dissolution of Conflict

Exercise on Pages 149/150

Type of Conflict	What is the Attachment?	How Would You Resolve?
1 **Disagreement**	You are attached to your opinion	Agree to disagree
2 **Misunderstanding**	You are attached to a perception of what you thought the other said and meant	Check your understanding by asking for clarity
3 **Blame for the Past**	You are attached to a memory of when you believed they hurt your feelings	Let go of the memory - realise they did not hurt your feelings, you did!
4 **Personality Clash**	You are attached to how you want them to be	Accept them as they are
5 **Resistance to Authority**	You are attached to your belief that your ideas and ways are better	Offer your ideas and then step away and have no concern whether they are accepted or adopted
6 **Unmet Expectations of Another**	You are attached to your expectations	Have expectations but don't make your happiness dependent on them
7 **Position, Power or Privileges are Perceived to be Threatened**	You are attached to position, power and privileges	Share your power, position and privileges with others as much as possible

Going Forward

There are five basic practices that allow you to generate your own AHA moments, 'see' for your self and then integrate your insights to create new behaviours.

The Wisdom of MEDITATION

This is the journey to the heart of your being, to the core of your consciousness. This is not a place you go, it's a vibration of your consciousness in which you 'be'. That's where you always find your peace, your capacity to be loving and your own quiet joy! These are your natural states. No one can ever take them away. Whenever we construct an identity out of what we are not we temporarily lose our ability to be in those states.

Many of us also develop the tendency to be absent. It's the habit of living in memories of the past or in speculations about the future. We don't notice we are missing our life in the present. As you practice some form or meditation you are gradually unlearning the habit of 'drifting' and the natural ability to stay in 'present moment awareness' is restored.

The Wisdom of CONTEMPLATION

But meditation is not enough. Just as consuming the images in a beautifully illustrated book can seem to be satisfying, it's only when their meaning is understood that their beauty then has depth and significance. So too it's necessary to realize for your self why and how you created those many self-sabotaging habits within your consciousness in the first place. Why certain feelings and emotions are arising regularly. Why your mind is the 'arena of creation' within you and how to use your mind in more creative and accurate ways. Why your intellect is often fast asleep or easily led or just plain tired, and how to refresh it.

Contemplation is a combination of looking at and seeing behind your thoughts and feelings, desires and resistances. Seeing their source, significance and their meaning. It can also include reflecting on the insights and wisdom of others. They also offer many signposts and indicators that can help you to understand what is happening within your consciousness, within your self.

The Wisdom of APPLICATION

Once realization occurs the challenge is to bring it through from conscious intention and into behavior e.g. when there is the realization that love is what you are, and that love is also your purpose, it becomes clear that your relationships are both the opportunity and the context in which to give that love as care, as compassion, as forgiveness, as acceptance and many other 'forms'.   Each day provides many opportunities to practice applying what you realize to be true for you.

The Wisdom of CONTRIBUTION

During the process and practice of mediation the motivation behind all that you think and do becomes clearer. You start to see that your intentions fall into one of two categories. They are either giving or taking, benevolent or self-serving.

Wanting and taking simply become habitual, reactive responses within many of our relationships with people and circumstances. Even when we believe we are giving/caring, at a deeper level we are often out for our self! The more you restore your natural inclination to give, to be generous, to be kind, to serve others before our self, the weaker the habits of wanting, taking and possessing become. The misery (fear in the form of anxiety) that such acquisitive habits once brought with them, subsides.

The Wisdom of Keeping Good COMPANY

The company that you keep has an influence on your consciousness i.e. on what you think about, what feelings you generate and what attitudes you nourish. It pays to be with people who prefer to connect and converse on subjects such as self-awareness and self-understanding.

There is a mutual nourishment when you are with people who are deeply interested in cultivating greater clarity about all the topics featured in this book. Not in an obsessive way, but in a way that you encourage each other to deepen your understanding of what it means to be your self and live wisely and calmly in a world that seems to becoming faster and more superficial by the day.

There is no one right way to combine such practices, only your way. And that will likely vary from day-to-day, week-to-week, alongside your many other priorities. None are compulsory, all have value.

Mike George

Mike is a senior member of the faculty of Cotrugli Business School

As a management tutor, facilitator and coach his specialist areas include Personal and Executive Development, Liberating Leadership and Managing with Emotional Intelligence.

He is an author of 14 books focused on enhancing self-awareness, emotional intelligence and personal enlightenment.

www.mikegeorgebooks.com

www.relax7.com

or email

mike@relax7.com

"Don't judge each day by the harvest you reap
but by the seeds that you plant."
Robert Louis Stevenson

Cotrugli Business School

COTRUGLI Business School headquarters are located in Zagreb and Belgrade, with branch offices in Sofia, Bucharest, Ljubljana, Podgorica and Dubai. Through these regional operational centers, COTRUGLI is creating Alumni networks in Bulgaria, Bosnia and Herzegovina, Croatia, Macedonia, Montenegro, Romania, Slovenia and Serbia, while at the same time reaching cultures and business environments worldwide.

In addition to MBA programs, COTRUGLI is specialized in delivering customized In House programs and Open Enrollment programs. Collaboration with the world's leading experts and more than 11,000 of satisfied clients has greatly contributed to the affirmation of the School as the most progressive in the SEE region.

COTRUGLI Business School has been awarded the AMBA accreditation for its MBA programs. Association of MBAs provides independent proof of quality and excellence for MBA programs. AMBA's goal is to constantly develop and enhance the quality of MBA programs worldwide. Among thousands of business schools worldwide, only 200 have been AMBA accredited. Some of them are IMD (Switzerland), IESE (Spain), London Business School, INSEAD (France) and COTRUGLI Business School.

Zagreb: Buzinski prilaz 10, 10010, Zagreb, Croatia

Phone: +385 1 3706 270

Belgrade: Visegradska, Beograd, Serbia

Phone: +381 69 1190903

Lightning Source UK Ltd.
Milton Keynes UK
UKHW02f0944080618
323935UK00009B/510/P